50 Reproducible Activities for Promoting Ethics within the Organization

by

Dr. Marlene Caroselli

HRD Press • Amherst • Massachusetts

Published by: HRD Press
                  22 Amherst Road
                  Amherst, MA 01002
                  800-822-2801 (U.S. and Canada)
                  413-253-3488
                  413-253-3490 (fax)
                  www.hrdpress.com

ISBN 978-1-61014-385-1

Production services by Jean Miller
Cover design by Eileen Klockars
Editorial work by Robie Grant

Table of Contents

Part B. Ethical Corporate Citizenship

Part C. Ethical Salesmanship

Part D. Ethical Management

Part E. Ethical Teamwork

Introduction

The headlines scream at us daily: "Thousands lose retirement funds in collapse of company." "Accounting firm shreds documents." "Top executive commits suicide as investigation widens." "President pardons tax evader." "Police officer admits taking bribe." "Priest confesses to murder." "Crematory operator faces 339 charges of theft by deception." "Quality of surgical facilities woefully inadequate." "Conflicts cloud objectivity of corporate boards." "Directors' conflicts of interest often buried deep in firms' SEC filings." "Buffett tells directors to really dog auditors."

Tyco, Enron, Adelphia, WorldCom, Arthur Andersen, Merrill Lynch, Imclone Systems, Global Crossing—the deeds and misdeeds of corporate officers have entered the shame-filled, scandal-filled pages that capture for history unethical misappropriations and misreporting of funds. Following these business meltdowns, change is finally under way. Corporate governance policies are being revisited, as are the methods corporations use to compensate their top executives. (Witness former CEO Jack Welch's decision to return his post-retirement perks to General Electric.) Many companies are contemplating, if not enforcing, the disclosure of executive stock plans and the treatment of stock options as expenses. (In the words of Warren Buffett, "The ratcheting up of compensation has been obscene.")

So common has been the breach of ethics by individuals and organizations in which we have placed our collective trust that the language has evolved new words to express our collective concern. "Institutional betrayal" is the phrase that denotes the destruction of faith that we once placed, without question, in organizations such as police forces, schools, churches, and bureaucratic organizations. As a nation, we are in the midst of an identity crisis, redefining the rules that once governed us individually and collectively.

Demands for reform are being made by the media, community members, activists, investors, stakeholders, Congress, employees, and the public at large. In fact, a survey by Dale Carnegie Training reported in *HR Fact Finder* ("Would You Blow the Whistle?" August 2002, page 6), finds 75% of business people surveyed would "blow the whistle" if they discovered bad management practices in their company.

Reforms will continue because of public outcries and Congressional investigations will continue. Securities laws are being overhauled; the New York Stock Exchange and the American Stock Exchange have proposed changes for closer regulation of corporate governance policies. The schism that once existed separated the soft world of ethics (often considered subjective) and the hard world of finance (considered objective and quantifiable) is closing. Corporate social responsibility (CSR) is a force behind that schism-closing, as systems are developed to make leaders accountable and to create a culture that fulfills its responsibilities. Activism and accountability are no longer strange bedfellows.

There are those who believe rules cannot make someone moral—a person is either ethical or not. To be sure, no course, no book, no training activity can convert an unethical person into an ethical one. You cannot "teach ethics." We believe this. And yet, living as we do in an Age of Paradox, we also believe:

- People may be engaged in activities they don't realize are unethical or illegal.
- Discussion and thought can create a cognitive dissonance that may lead to an altered state of behavior.
- Serious events can prompt serious shifts in perspective and action alike.
- One person can serve as a powerful force to offset the inertia born of long-standing practices.

For these reasons, we've compiled a series of activities for you to use as a training program in and of itself. These activities can also be used as elements within training you are already doing in the areas of general Leadership, Corporate Citizenship, Sales, Management, and Teamwork. The activities are designed to probe, to push, to prod, and to remove the calcified plaque that may have accumulated over time through repeated thoughts and actions. The activities in and of themselves may not effect sudden ethical behavior. However, they just might create a climate in which existing practices and policies can be examined. In time, it is hoped such examination will lead to an improved moral climate.

This is not a book to be used only by trainers, however. Anyone who serves in an official or unofficial position of leadership can employ these activities to stimulate thought and discussion regarding appropriate decisions/behaviors/words/actions. Supervisors can use the activities during staff meetings; team leaders can energize their process-improvement meetings; managers can distribute excerpts such as the monograph to department members; executive decision-makers can take some of the activities into account as they engage in strategic planning; editors of the organizational newsletter can use the quizzes as integrity-driven fillers for their publication.

Overview of the Book

50 Reproducible Activities for Promoting Ethics within the Organization is divided into five sections, each of which is introduced via an interview with a leading business ethicist. Among them are authors Nan DeMars, Laurie Haughey, and Kristen Arnold, consultant/coach Robin Wilson, and attorney Tom Mitrano. With their own unique perspectives, these contributors present both microcosmic and macrocosmic views of ethics at work. Excerpted, they can serve as thought-provocative material for anyone and everyone in the organization interested in ethical issues.

The five sections each have ten exercises designed to stimulate discussion and promote inquiry regarding business ethics. The activities focus on Leadership, Corporate Citizenship, Salesmanship, Management, and Teamwork. (Despite their placement in one section or another, many of these activities are "crossovers"—with just a little tweaking, you can adapt them to several other purposes.) Contributing to this collection is a wide range of trainers from a variety of disciplines and locations, including Europe, India, Canada, and a broad cross-section of the United States.

I. Activities to Promote Ethical Leadership

Is it possible to operate within the letter of the law and still do something questionable at best, unethical at worst? Many believe, for example, that President Clinton's pardon of billionaire Marc Rich represented just such a scenario. On the other hand, is it possible to break the law and be considered honorable for having done so? Perhaps even be honored for having done so? Such was the case with Dorie Miller, who was honored posthumously for having brought down enemy aircraft at Pearl Harbor. Dorie Miller was a black sailor. He broke the law of the land when he used weaponry labeled "For Whites Only."

This section promotes leadership, the kind of leadership that takes courage, commitment, and moral rectitude.

II. Activities to Promote Ethical Corporate Citizenship

Toynbee's Law of Progressive Simplifications states, "The measure of a civilization's growth and sustainable vitality lies in its ability to transfer increasing amounts of energy and attention from the material side of life to the educational, psychological, cultural, aesthetic, and spiritual side." It is this law that serves as the foundation for *50 Reproducible Activities for Promoting Ethics within the Organization,* for the root of all evil truly is money and, if not money, the need to acquire "more" than we have—more power, more favor, more material things that bespeak our power or wealth. This is as true on a personal level as it is on the organizational level. Think of some of the most scandalous ethical breaches in recent corporate history. Uncover the reason behind the ethical breach and you'll almost always find money or power at its core.

The activities in this section help participants examine their micro- and macro-motivation. They'll have opportunities to think about the power of ethical persuasion, the pros and cons of charisma, and choices and their consequences.

III. Activities to Promote Ethical Salesmanship

Whether it's an entire corporation, a sales division or department within that corporation, a single office, or an individual salesperson, the questions regarding business ethics cannot be answered without having definitions to serve as guidelines. We'll explore a number of issues that warrant the issuance of written definitions—issues such as values, goals, policies, and the very relationships the corporate body has to its suppliers, its shareholders, its competitors, its employees, and, of course, to its clients.

Participants will be engaged in this section in surveys, role-plays, and panel discussions.

IV. Activities to Promote Ethical Management

Ethical management involves, in part, the larger issues of being socially responsible. Even if your participants are not in the corporate echelon that decides what profits can be earmarked for charitable purposes, they can still consider issues such as energy conservation; creating a work culture free of "isms" like age-ism and sex-ism; environmental damage; diversity; and everyday issues involving honesty and integrity. Participants will be encouraged to do more than think, though: they'll be asked to undertake some grass-roots movements in support of these issues.

Small-group activities and self-assessments are included among the activities that explore situational ethics.

V. Activities to Promote Ethical Teamwork

"Truth, justice, and the American way" are some of the topics examined in this section, which explores both loyalty and divided loyalties that team members often have to face. In several exercises, participants will act as "paper-judges," ruling on real-world, real-workplace cases. In so doing, they'll learn to avoid the mistakes others have made in work conditions similar to their own. They'll also have an opportunity to compare their rulings with those of the court.

In addition to litigation scenarios, participants will engage in activities of a game-like nature, but activities with a serious intent: to engender ethical behavior by team members.

Overview of the Exercises

These exercises are diverse: Contributing authors vary in their backgrounds and locations. International trainers from the Netherlands, India, and Canada are represented, as are American trainers with a wide range of specialties and experience. In addition to exercises by the editor/author, other exercises have been submitted by academic leaders and entrepreneurial consultants.

The exercises range in duration from 10 minutes to an hour and a half. Each begins with the **Timeframe,** followed by an **Overview** and **Purpose**. The ideal **Group size** and the best **Room arrangement**, which can impact the amount of activity participants engage in and the degree of creativity they offer, are noted next. In the instructional construct, the required **Materials** and a step-by-step **Method** for executing the activity are listed. What makes the activities unique are the **Discussion** prompts, which enable the trainer to widen the exercise's application.

Similarly, the **Quotation** in each activity can be used in the following ways:

- ✓ Post the quotations around the room and encourage participants to view and discuss them during breaks.

- ✓ Ask table group leaders to select a favorite quote posted around the room and discuss it within their groups.

- ✓ Write a given quote on the flipchart (or put it on an overhead transparency) and use it as a stimulus for whole-class discussion.

- ✓ Select two quotes that imply contradiction and call on two different participants to explain/substantiate the differing viewpoints.

- ✓ Ask table groups to share examples of their own experiences as they relate to various quotes.

- ✓ Compile the quotes and distribute the sheet to participants. Periodically during the training day, call on someone to share his or her favorite quote and the relevance it has for that person.

Scattered throughout the activities are **Variations**, alternative ways of presenting the material or expanding its applicability. The **Points of Interest** present relevant research and material that can easily be incorporated into the exercises.

Overview of the Methodologies

A deliberately wide array of methodologies is employed within these activities, in view of the facts that:

- ✓ Adults used to multitasking need to switch their attention and focus from one kind of activity to another every 15 or 20 minutes.

- ✓ Dry and prolonged lectures do not appeal to adult learners as much as interactive, hands-on exercises in which they can do more than merely listen.

- ✓ Because some view the training experience as one fraught with danger, i.e., their reputations and competence are on display, these exercises have success virtually built-in. Some are done privately, such as the assessments. Others are done in groups. Group assignments lessen the "exposure" of any one participant. And, many of the assignments have neither right nor wrong answers—merely ideas to be explored. (Group discussions, for example, encourage the exchange of ideas.) We do recommend the trainer begin the day with an encouragement to participate but with the acknowledgement that some may prefer not to and that preference will be honored.

- ✓ Each of us has a preferred learning modality. Some of the methodologies are designed for visual intake, others for auditory, still others for tactile expression. Coupled with traditional classroom alternatives—video, flipcharts, and overhead transparencies—these exercises will enhance the typical learner's ability to absorb and retain ideas.

You'll find considerable flexibility with these exercises. Some can be used as ice-breakers; others as energizers; still others as a medium for transferring knowledge via the written word. Some are designed to be taken back to the workplace and shared with colleagues. Some are designed to develop awareness; some diagnose; some develop documents that can be used on the job; some work to establish an ethical congruence between what is right and what is being done; some stimulate discussion, and some are simply enjoyable excursions into the world of ideas. All, though, have this in common—they are easy to use *and* they have a solid instructional core from which an ethical power can be released.

While the collection is primarily designed for use by trainers, its use is not limited to trainers. These exercises can be used by team leaders, supervisors, managers, and employees at any level. In other words, anyone interested in promoting an ethical culture and/or assuming a leadership role in continuous improvement will find in these pages numerous ideas that, when implemented, will truly make a difference.

Participant Assignments: Dyads, triads, teams, and whole-group exercises are used to achieve various purposes. When the exercise calls for some type of revelation or personal experience, the dyad or other small-group formation is suggested. When role-plays are used or other exercises calling for an observer to note an interpersonal exchange, we suggest using triads. When an exercise merits full-group attention, the method incorporates speaking to the class as a whole, throughout a given exercise or for any one part of it.

Quizzes: The element of surprise can be a powerful force in retaining new knowledge. Many of the quizzes are designed to both elucidate and educate. By juxtaposing what they knew pre-quiz to what they learned post-quiz, participants can more quickly appreciate the width of the knowledge gap. Other quizzes are simply designed to test the degree of retention or to determine the degree of comprehension. (We recommend you never ask any one participant how he or she scored on a given quiz. Additionally, never ask for a show of hands related to scores at the lower end of the continuum.)

Handouts: These are designed to supplement the intent of the exercise and to reinforce the main points being made. Handouts are also employed when participants need to have a common understanding of a situation, on the basis of which they'll take further action. Many of these handouts are designed with "portability" in mind—i.e., it's our hope that participants will take them back to the office and share them with colleagues.

Case Studies: Case studies, due to their real-world nature, enable participants to correlate their own experiences to someone else's and to project possible outcomes. When the actual outcomes are compared to their projections, participants can then learn through discussion and analysis how best to handle comparable situations if and when they occur in their own lives. There's a safety net associated with case studies—they reveal pitfalls without making participants take the actual steps into those pits. By studying how someone else did or should have handled a difficult situation, participants can derive benefit that can later be applied to their own personal and professional situations.

Buzz Groups/Small Groups: There's a definite "buzz" that emanates from a classroom filled with small groups working on the same assignment and probably approaching it from different perspectives. Trainers can optimize the excitement by establishing a few ground rules, among them the time element and the fact that groups should try to keep their voices down so that others can work more easily. Additional factors to be considered include the following:

- *Selection of group participants*: To avoid having people who work together all day sit together all day in a training session, here are several possibilities for grouping (or re-grouping):

  ✓ Match well-known business titles with their authors. (In a group of 20 participants, you'd have 10 titles and 10 authors.)

  ✓ As participants enter, give each a different colored candy kiss. Then assemble groups based on their colors.

  ✓ Write the name of the course on three large sheets of heavy paper or cardboard—each sheet will have the course name. Divide each sheet into irregular puzzle-pieces (seven or eight pieces for each puzzle if class size, for example, is 22). Cut the pieces for each sheet and put them in an envelope. Shake the pieces up and then distribute one to each participant who enters the door. Groups form on the basis of assembled pieces.

- *Selection of group leader*: To avoid having the most vocal person always serve as the group leader or reporter (and to have the recorder always be a woman "with neat handwriting"), rotate the assignment as follows:

  ✓ Issue directions such as: "The person with the longest hair will be the reporter this time."

  ✓ Make this request: "Raise your hands with one finger protruding… preferably the little finger. Now, as you lower your hands, let the finger point to the person at your table whom you wish to be your group leader."

  ✓ Ask participants to figure out who has been with the organization for the longest period of time. That person becomes the group recorder.

- *Reports*: Group after group delivering an oral report, all day long, can be soporific. Consider these alternatives:

  ✓ Appoint a roving reporter who will circulate among the groups, sitting in just long enough to gain a sense of their discussions. The reporter then gives a brief overview of each group's discussion, allowing limited input from the groups to update or amend any of the reporter's comments.

  ✓ Have each group prepare a one-paragraph report on flipchart paper. You will then read each of the posted paragraphs.

  ✓ Challenge the group spokespersons to submit their reports in a creative fashion: a rhyme, an alliterative phrase, or even a rap song.

Guided Discussions: These activities are predicated on monographs that participants read in class. (Ideally, these can be distributed prior to the class so that valuable class time need not be spent on the reading. The advance arrangement also prevents the "lag" that results from people reading at different rates.) Once the group has internalized the material, you'll discuss it with questions that have been prepared ahead of time.

Scripts: Scripts bring out the creativity in participants. They also provoke insights and help participants convert theory to practical applications. Scripts have a way of sharpening the distinctions between best-case and worst-case scenarios and provide an interesting alternative to direct discussions of a given point. (Note: Scripts need not always be enacted. Often, the mere exploration of ideas on paper is sufficient to illustrate the point.)

Role-Play: You'll find some participants naturally hesitant to engage in role-plays. It's important to overcome that reluctance, though, because role-plays provide an instructional value provided by no other method. Reluctance is usually tied to tension—a tension that results when individuals think about being someone or something other than themselves. If unchecked, tension can stultify creativity and can even block the natural flow of ideas. One simple and quick way to relieve tension is the Y-E-S technique: Have the entire group engage in a deep, satisfying, collective **Y**awn just prior to the role-plays. Then provide **E**ducation about the value of role-plays: they help participants prepare for real-world encounters, they illustrate significant points, and they can actually be fun. Also provide education regarding the specific parameters of the roles and of the exercise itself. Finally, provide a few moments of **S**ilence, during which they can collect their thoughts (perhaps even jot down a few notes). Then…let the role-plays begin.

Assessments: If it weren't for training opportunities, some participants would never introspect. The training environment is ideal for encouraging participants to take time to consider questions with potentially far-reaching implications. The assessments provided as part of some exercises invite self- and organizational-analysis.

Panels: An interesting variation on the theme of knowledge-acquisition is the use of panels. Panels can be composed of "outsiders," who are invited to the training room to present their views on a given topic. Following this presentation, a question-and-answer session will bring effective closure to the event.

Panels, though, can also be composed of participants—either volunteers or spokespersons selected by their table groups to present summaries of the work groups have just completed. Panel members, representing the class as a whole, can exchange ideas on behalf of their groups. (An alternative would be to have participants write additional questions for panel members and to have a moderator collect these and present them to the panel for response.)

Fishbowls: This technique involves having one group work in the center of the room while the remainder of the class sits in a wider circle around them, observing their interactions. It's quite effective, for example, for the inside group to participate in a team meeting while the outside group observes their interactions and their effectiveness in accomplishing a given task.

A Final Note

It would be remiss of us not to mention the ethical obligations you have as a trainer, especially a trainer of business ethics. At the risk of offending veteran trainers, but as an important checklist for new trainers, we include here a list of responsibilities/recommendations that bespeak both professionalism and an ethical commitment to the profession. (Ideally, most of the following behaviors are already part of your professional persona.)

- ✓ I know this subject well enough to be considered something of an expert in it.

- ✓ I get to the room at least half an hour early to set it up and to greet early arrivals.

- ✓ I do all I can to make participants feel welcome, including the placement of a welcome sign on the door or the writing of the word on the flipchart.

- ✓ I begin with an introduction of the course and its purpose, of myself and my credentials for teaching the course, and then with introductions of the participants themselves.

- ✓ I present an overview or agenda of what the course entails.

- ✓ I make a sincere effort to remember names of the participants.

- ✓ I periodically review the material or provide summaries.

- ✓ I consciously avoid sarcasm, vulgarity, inappropriate humor, and references that may be offensive.

- ✓ I anticipate questions that will arise and prepare responses to them.

- ✓ I employ anecdotes to illustrate points.

- ✓ I assure participants they will never be made to feel uncomfortable.

- ✓ I never lecture for more than 15 minutes at a stretch.

- ✓ I incorporate humor into the presentation.

- ✓ I include relevant news events and statistics in my presentation.

✓ I am physical with knowledge—i.e., make dramatic gestures from time to time.

✓ I provide a change of pace on a regular basis.

✓ I consciously think about ways to make the presentations interactive.

✓ I encourage participants to meet and work with others in the room.

✓ I invite feedback about the presentation.

✓ I strive to relate the material to participants' jobs and missions.

✓ I attempt to learn as much as I can about participants and their organizations.

✓ I schedule breaks as needed.

✓ I ensure the screen and flipchart can be seen by every participant.

✓ I keep abreast of developments in the field.

✓ I revise my materials on a continual basis.

✓ I provide professional-looking handouts and references.

✓ I employ a wide variety of methodologies.

✓ I invite questions and feedback on my presentation.

✓ I invite (but put limits on) the telling of "war stories."

✓ I make myself available to participants.

✓ I provide ways for participants to be continuous learners.

✓ I design effective closure.

Part A:
Ethical Leadership
Introduction: Laurie Haughey

Teaching Ethical Leadership: The Collaborative Model

"The problems and needs confronting our schools and communities are far too complex for unilateral, and largely random, action and independent actors, no matter how well intentioned. It's become cliché to note that it takes a whole village to raise a child; but, make no mistake about it, the successful public leaders of the twenty-first century will be those most skilled at building villages."

> From Hank Rubin, *Collaborative Leadership: Building Partnerships for Effective Schools and Communities*, Corwin Press, May 2002

For years, colleges and universities like Clemson University have been teaching business ethics. The course is a prerequisite for graduation from the school of business. And yet, for a lesson in ethical leadership, one need not venture into the classroom, but instead take note of the rising number of college presidents and chancellors who have adopted the most ethical form of leadership—a collaborative leadership style. This style of leadership, when properly applied, is a boon for the leader who uses it—especially in a college setting where people are employed to think aloud. But in the spirit of education, let's think for a while about what the world of business could learn from encouraging its employees to cross-pollinate ideas, solutions, and innovations.

While the recent downturn in the economy has thrown industry and manufacturing into a tailspin, and CEOs like Kenneth Lay are being asked serious questions on Capitol Hill, Clemson University's president, Jim Barker, is resolved to employ all of the school's collective wisdom to solve the problems brought on by a state-wide budget cut. Unlike most of his counterparts in industry, however, Jim Barker used the problem of a budget cut to strengthen the common resolve of the university community. While he kept everyone informed through brown-bag lunches and town meetings, he asked every employee for support and problem-solving. What he got was commitment and a solution. In a recent e-mail to employees, he commended them on their spirit of resolve, adding that without their contribution of thought, "we might have been less bold and aggressive when faced with the prospect of a 15 percent state budget cut…we might not have developed the Road Map."

13

Using collaborative leadership to solve the budget cut allowed the president of Clemson University to pull in top experts in their fields from no more than an 800-yard radius! In the meantime, he remained focused on the overall mission of the university and its unique 10-year goals. As a result, the university goals remained unchanged—the obstacle of funding cuts providing an interesting *underdog mentality* on campus. The greatest advantage, of course, is that everyone loves an underdog.

More importantly, as a leader with several leadership styles at his disposal, Jim Barker's choice provided the winning example that collaboration evokes. Collaboration creates a greater sense of ownership of the situation while at the same time creating a democratic, inclusive environment of troubleshooters and problem solvers. When a leader provides the example of successful collaboration, the results become contagious. In fact, recently the university's governing accreditation board, the Southern Association of Colleges and Schools (SACS), awarded the school two commendations, dubbing Clemson "a ministry of listening," and acknowledging the exemplary collaboration among the vice presidents of academics, public service, and research.

In Newman's *The Idea of a University*, he calls on university leaders to create schools that are "a direct preparation for this world," embracing the responsibility of properly equipping students with the necessary values and traits to thrive in the "inevitable" world outside. Though written in 1854, Newman's vision of the role of universities is timeless. No institution or individual owns the patent on knowledge. Rather, due to the limitless nature of knowledge, each institution of higher education needs to send forth its graduates under the common motto: explore, exhaust, exchange. Tomorrow's leaders must witness presidents of universities, elected officials, and leaders from industry practicing what I call the three handsome sisters: *collaborative leadership, forthright, informed communication,* and *life-long learning.*

Higher education's example of collaborative leadership has broad applications for the world of work, to which our universities ultimately send their students. In that world—as the events of September 11 so tragically taught us—expertise and inter-unit collaboration are critical. Pilots are trained now in security; flight attendants know martial arts; passengers will probably never again simply sit and watch events unfold. Still, even before this tragedy, collaborative leadership projects were underway between corporations and schools; buyers and sellers; hospitals and patients. Whenever and wherever vision is aligned with ethical collaboration, multilevel advantages ensue.

Just as in education, the strength of business lies not in solid leadership alone but also sound succession planning. As accomplished a CEO as he was, Lee Ioccoca did not have the answers to every problem and was not the sole innovator at Chrysler. In fact, the two greatest strengths in adopting a collaborative leadership style are that, one, it belies the notion that a single mind has the answers to every situation, and second, it encourages grooming leadership from the top down and across an organization. In his book, *Good to Great: Why Some Companies Make the Leap...and Others Don't*, Jim Collins indentifies Chrysler in the "unsustained" category when looking at the variety of companies used in his study. Studying Chrysler under Ioccoca, he found that the company followed "a pattern we found in every unsustained comparison: a spectacular rise under a tyrannical disciplinarian, followed by an equally spectacular decline when the disciplinarian stepped away, leaving behind no enduring culture of discipline...." One might argue that Chrysler faltered without Ioccoca at the helm because he had failed to practice collaborative leadership to the point that a proper succession plan was devised.

To its credit in higher education, the collaborative leadership style provides the environment to reap the full benefits of merging schools of thought. After all, would anyone have ever heard of John Nash the mathematician? It took an economist to partner his knowledge to Nash's mathematical model to give it the value of a Nobel Prize. There are many schools making the investment in time to promote collaborative endeavors. For example, at the University of Massachusetts, Sherry H. Penney holds an endowed chair in the College of Management. Her charge is to establish a Center for Collaborative Leadership. At the same time, Texas Instruments has offered $3 million in funding to members of its DSP Leadership University. In everyone's view, partnering Texas Instruments with the Georgia Institute of Technology, Rice University, and MIT will drive innovations in the field and promote research and education at each institution.

It is only natural that institutions of higher education embrace collaborative work. Whereas industrialists often say, "There is much work to do," I believe that Shakespeare's Hamlet best expressed the humbling endeavor facing educators, researchers, and scholars when he exclaimed, "There are more things in Heaven and Earth, Horatio, than are dreamt of in your philosophy" (*Hamlet* 1.5.166 – 167). Collaborative endeavors allow us to remain undaunted by the enormity of the task while showing students the power of partnerships. As teachers to the next generation of thinkers, we must ask ourselves: What more could we know—which inventions, medical breakthroughs, illustrious business ventures, and inspirations to the creative arts lie just one intelligent conversation away?

Collins, Jim. *Good to Great: Why Some Companies Make the Leap… and Others Don't.* New York: Harper Collins Publishers, Inc., 2001.

Newman, Cardinal John Henry. *The Idea of a University.* Ed. Martin J. Svaglic. Notre Dame, Indiana: University of Notre Dame, 1982.

Submitted by: Laurie Haughey
Clemson University
341 Sirrine Hall
Clemson, South Carolina 29634
Phone: 864-656-3991
Fax: 864-656-7351
E-mail: Hlaurie@clemson.edu
Web site: www.clemson.edu/success

Laurie Haughey is the author *of Athletes Off the Field: A Model for Team Building and Leadership Development Through Service Learning.* Employed by Clemson University since 1989, she serves as Conference Organizer/Training Development Director in the university's Department of Off-Campus, Distance and Continuing Education. Laurie, a former track and field student athlete, earned degrees in English and Sociology from Clemson. She has dedicated her career—in academics and earlier in athletics—to promoting lifelong learning and collaborative endeavors that serve to build each participant's leadership experience. While working in athletics as an academic advisor, Laurie initiated a peer leadership group among the football student athletes. Leaders In Football and Education, a.k.a. LIFE LINE, completes ten service learning projects each year and works in partnership with elementary schools and other service-missioned charity groups. Laurie is the former president of Clemson's Letterman's Association.

1. Ethical Leadership
Intelligent Life in the Universe

Approximately 15 minutes

PURPOSE
To prompt discussion about the need for leaders to provide evidence of an ethical foundation on which their platforms are constructed.

GROUP SIZE
Any size group, ideally divided into groups of four or five.

ROOM ARRANGEMENT
If possible, table groups for four or five participants.

MATERIALS
- Equipment for displaying PowerPoint slides
- Slide 1.1, *"The Surest Sign"*
- Slide 1.1, *"The Surest Sign"* (concluded)
- Slide 1.2, *"Sure Signs"*
- Slide 1.3, *"Signs"*

PROCEDURE
1. Begin by asking how many read the cartoon strip "Calvin and Hobbes." (**Note:** If possible, cut out several "Calvin and Hobbes" cartoons from the newspaper or a book and distribute one to each table. Allow a few minutes for the cartoon to be read.)

2. State that the cartoon's originator, Bill Watterson, has a line that you find amusing. Display Slide 1.1 and read aloud: "The surest sign that intelligent life exists elsewhere in the universe is…"

3. Ask groups to come up with two or three completions for this sentence opening. Allow no more than 5 minutes for the assignment.

4. Have a spokesperson from each group share the group's favorite line.

5. Next, display Slide 1.1 (concluded), revealing Bill Watterson's "punch line."

6. Display Slide 1.2 and ask small groups to decide on a leader whose actions they can analyze. This could be an organizational leader in their own firm or a different organization; it could be a state leader, a national leader, or an international leader. Once they've determined what leader to consider, have them find three specific things they believe manifest ethical behavior in that leader. This portion of the exercise will take about 10 minutes.

7. Have participants work alone to complete Slide 1.3, the final slide, which asks them to think about ways they demonstrate adherence to ethical standards.

8. Finally, ask them to work in pairs or triads to discuss their thoughts.

VARIATION

Ask for volunteers to write an article for a management publication (or their own organizational newsletters) based on the vitally important connections between leadership and ethical behavior.

In courses dealing with Conflicts in the Workplace, the trainer is bound to cite the need for developing and maintaining mutual respect. That respect is often dependent on ethical behaviors; the erosion of that respect and of trust is often related to the absence of ethical behaviors or—worse yet—the manifestation of *un*ethical behaviors.

DISCUSSION

- Is it ethical for a leader to deliberately find ways to demonstrate his or her ethics?

- Is it possible for a given action to be viewed as both ethical and unethical by two different people or groups? If so, what examples can you think of?

- Is there a danger for a leader who makes his or her intents and intentions known?

QUOTATION

"I have learnt silence from the talkative, toleration from the intolerant, and kindness from the unkind; yet strange, I am ungrateful to these teachers."
– Kahlil Gibran

POINTS OF INTEREST

One of the most flagrant examples of unethical behavior is the violation of federal copyright laws. Duplicating software violates Section 17 of that law. Advise others that the only legal reason for copying a program is for an individual's reliance on a backup disk. Individuals who break this law could be fined $25,000, could be imprisoned, or could have both consequences applied.

Slide 1.1

The Surest Sign

"The surest sign that intelligent
life exists elsewhere in the
universe is...

1.1

Slide 1.1 (concluded)

The Surest Sign

"The surest sign that intelligent
life exists elsewhere in the
universe is...

...that it has never tried to contact
us!"

1.1 (concluded)

Slide 1.2

> Sure signs that ethical leadership exists in
>
> our _____
>
> are _____;
>
> and _____.
>
> 1.2

Slide 1.3

> Sure signs that my own leadership is
>
> ethical include _____
>
> _____;
>
> and _____.
>
> 1.3

2. Ethical Leadership
You're Better Ough

Approximately 30 minutes

OVERVIEW

The numerous pronunciations of the *"ough"* syllable (including the sound of "off," as in "You're better off") form the basis of this exercise, which encourages leaders to consider the multiple perspectives from which their actions may be viewed.

PURPOSE

To develop the essential leadership ability that involves considering several viewpoints that could be applied to a given situation.

GROUP SIZE

Any size group. Participants will first work in triads and then in groups of six. A spokesperson from each group will participate in a panel discussion.

ROOM ARRANGEMENT

If possible, flexible seating so that triads can be formed, and later, seats can be arranged for an audience to face a panel of presenters.

MATERIALS
- Flipchart and marking pens
- Equipment for displaying PowerPoint slides
- Slide 2.1, *"You're Better Ough"*
- Handout 2.1, *"Two Sides to Every Story"*

PROCEDURE
1. Begin with a brain teaser for participants, who are seated in triads: How many words can they think of that contain different pronunciations of the combined letters "ough"? (**Option:** Challenge them to create a sentence with the various words.)

2. Call on a spokesperson from each group to share the words they've thought of.

3. Write the words on a flipchart, noting that a given combination of letters is subject to numerous possible pronunciations, depending on the words selected.

4. Show Slide 2.1 and compare the pronunciations with those on the flipchart.

5. Segue from the brain teaser to the fact that a leader's actions can be viewed from various points along a wide spectrum of possibilities. And, each interpreter may believe (perhaps rightly) that his or her interpretation is correct.

6. Distribute the handout and ask triads to join another triad to form a team of six. The team will discuss the questions on the handout.

7. Have a spokesperson from each team come forward to sit at a table. The individuals on this panel will present the viewpoints held by their team. You will moderate and will invite questions from the audience.

8. Conclude by announcing the actual judgment: the court (the United States Court of Appeals for the Ninth Circuit) sided with the employee. Their interpretation was based on several facts: the manager was a veteran employee, and so it was reasonable for the employee to trust his word. Further, that "word" was not a casual or unauthorized statement. The court held that the promise constituted an enforceable employment contract, especially given the formal nature in which that promise was uttered.

In the interest of fairness to all concerned, HR policies should spell out the conditions involved with personnel changes. If your organization does not have such policies in effect, assume a leadership position and begin to codify the consequences of changes so that fair and ethical treatment will ensue.

VARIATION
Try this experiment with the group to illustrate how the same event can elicit different accounts from various individuals, each of whom is probably certain that his or her version is the accurate one. Plan to have a colleague who is not familiar to the class participants enter the room and ask for the flipchart (or overhead or some other common object). You will pretend not to know this individual and will politely protest, stating that you had arranged for the equipment and need it to present your program. The colleague will become more belligerent and insistent and will finally just pick up your equipment and take it out of the room with a few choice words and a loud slam of the door. Express your shock to the group and enlist their help: say that you intend to report the incident and have them describe exactly what happened. Collect the reports and have a volunteer analyze them for similarities and differences.

DISCUSSION
- Have you ever argued with someone who saw the same thing you saw (or heard the same thing you heard) and yet had an entirely different interpretation of the event? If so, recall the details.

- What advantages can you cite when a multiplicity of viewpoints surround a given event? What disadvantages?

- How can a leader best make use of the diversity of thought associated with his or her cause or proposal?

QUOTATION

"Before you speak, listen. Before you write, think. Before you spend, earn. Before you invest, investigate. Before you criticize, wait. Before you pray, forgive. Before you quit, try. Before you retire, save. Before you die, give."

– William A. Ward

POINTS OF INTEREST

Note that typically a casual remark cannot be regarded as the equivalent of terms in an employment contract. However, this situation contained more than a casual remark. The setting was formal, the prompt was a specific question asked by the employee, and a promise was made—more than once, in fact. In the actual case, the promise was made in front of a witness, further weakening the company's position.

Slide 2.1

A ploughman with a face like dough and hands rough as sandpaper, thoughtfully listened to the song "Scarborough Fair." Soon, though, he slipped into a slough of reverie, in which he coughed, hiccoughed, and then fell gently asleep.

2.1

Handout 2.1
Two Sides to Every Story

Situation

Susan Atkins worked on the assembly line at an automotive parts factory. Although she occasionally experienced tedium with the job, she liked it nonetheless, especially the benefits and good wages guaranteed by her union contract. One day her boss of 12 years, Anthony Trotto, called her in and said he was planning to reclassify her job to one that was not covered by the contract. In the next few weeks, Susan met several times with Mr. Trotto and asked each time about job security. She was repeatedly assured that her job was secure and as long as she continued to work well, she wouldn't have a problem. Unfortunately, Susan's ratings began moving toward the "unacceptable" range and she was ultimately fired.

Questions

1. If you had been Susan, would you have sued?

2. If so, on what grounds?

3. If you were the automotive company, what would your defense have been?

4. Can an oral assurance be considered a contract?

5. If so, what assurances have you made lately?

6. How would they hold up in court?

7. How do you think the court actually ruled in this case?

3. Ethical Leadership
Take Offense and Take the Offensive

Approximately 25 minutes

OVERVIEW
Ethical leaders have a fine sense of justice. They take offense when it deserves to be taken and then go on the offensive to ensure offensive actions are not repeated. This exercise uses real-world scenarios to stimulate discussion regarding those actions.

PURPOSE
- To heighten participants' awareness of inappropriate behavior.
- To caution against the use of certain negative-impact words.
- To stimulate thought regarding appropriate actions to be taken as a result of inappropriate behavior.

GROUP SIZE
Any size group. Participants will first work alone and then in pairs. The exercise concludes with a full-group discussion.

ROOM ARRANGEMENT
No special requirements.

MATERIALS
Handout 3.1, *"Your Reaction/Your Reply?"*

PROCEDURE
1. Distribute the handout and begin this exercise by pointing out that certain words are obviously offensive to various groups. Surprisingly, though, not every person within a given group finds a given word offensive. Some women, for example, don't mind being referred to as "girls"; others take immediate umbrage. Still, it's best to avoid those words and phrases that are well-recognized as insulting.

2. Point out that it's the leader's ethical responsibility to create a workplace environment that is free from prejudice of any kind. Employees have a right not to be disparaged, mocked, insulted, threatened, or offended.

27

3. Next, explain that sometimes we employ an expression without realizing that it might sound prejudicial or insulting. The handout will explore four actual incidents. Participants will respond to the four incidents and will then share their thoughts with a partner.

4. Transition next to references based on current events (President Bush's declaration of the war against terrorism as a "crusade," for example) or to examples elicited from participants regarding similar incidents.

5. Conclude the exercise by leading a discussion (and, ideally, recording the results) that explores things an organizational leader/manager can and should do to ensure employees are treated respectfully.

VARIATION
This exercise can be easily adapted for programs emphasizing cultural diversity, conflict in the workplace, leadership, and communication skills.

DISCUSSION
- What, specifically, can a leader do to ensure offensive remarks are kept out of the workplace?

- What is the downside of being too politically correct?

- Can you think of instances in which a national figure was criticized/chastised for making seemingly innocent remarks?

- If you had made such a remark, in all innocence, would you feel compelled to apologize for it?

- How do First Amendment rights impinge on remarks that might cause offense?

QUOTATION
"The best effect of fine persons is felt after we have left their presence."
– Ralph Waldo Emerson

POINTS OF INTEREST
In the case of *Dan Antoni vs. Employment Security Department of the State of Washington,* No. 15764-4-III, the court ruled that Bonnie Showalter, who had been fired for being rude to customers, was entitled to benefits denied her when she was terminated. The court agreed the behavior was inappropriate but that it did not constitute misconduct—even though her boss had been told he would lose his licensing subagency if such behavior continued. Ms. Showalter claimed a strict diet caused her to "veer out of control." This claim ran counter to the definition of misconduct: which means a "willful act."

Handout 3.1
Your Reaction/Your Reply?

Directions
Decide what, if anything, you would have said or done if you had been the person to whom the offensive, albeit innocently offensive, remark was directed. Be prepared to explain the rationale behind your decision to say/do something or nothing.

Situation #1
Jeannette Guzman was engaged in a discussion of multitasking consulting at the annual office party. She excused herself at one point and headed to the hors d'oeuvres table, where she was approached by another employee who "complimented" her with these words: *"Jeannette, I just have to tell you how much I enjoyed listening to you just now. You are so intelligent... for a Mexican."*

Situation #2
Donna Silverstein was having a birthday lunch with four co-workers, when one of them admired her handbag, asking where she had purchased it. Donna recalled that she had purchased it when she was in Morocco, at an outdoor casbah. *"Oh,"* the other woman asked, clearly interested, *"did you have to Jew down the merchant to get it?"*

Situation #3
It's the first day on the job for Chynna Kim. One of her fellow workers, in an effort to welcome her, walks up, extends his hand, and jovially observes: *"I see they've hired another Chink."*

Situation #4
Linda Karolla (nee Giordano) has just transferred to a new department. The other secretaries took her to lunch to help orient her to the department. One of them cautions her: *"Mr. Martiello heads Accounting and he has very strict standards. He would never actually gyp anyone out of their money, but if anyone tries to gyp him, he just might call in the Mafia!"*

4. Ethical Leadership
Standing on Common Ground

Approximately 20 minutes

OVERVIEW
This brain teaser encourages critical thinking about the attributes of ethical leaders. Participants first identify such attributes and then engage in a mental challenge designed to elicit critical thinking in general terms.

OBJECTIVES
To generate insight and discussion regarding the attributes of ethical leaders.

GROUP SIZE
Any number of participants can engage in this exercise.

ROOM ARRANGEMENT
No special arrangements required.

MATERIALS
- Flipchart and marking pens
- Handout 4.1, *"Standing on Common Ground"*
- **Optional:** Provide token prizes for the winning pair, such as a paperback book about critical thinking or perhaps crossword puzzles from the daily newspaper.

PROCEDURES
1. Ask participants to think about the most ethical leader they have ever known or known about. Elicit examples from the group.

2. Then ask them to think about the specific attributes (mention "critical thinking" in particular, as an example) that the individual displayed or specific actions he or she took. List these on the flipchart as participants share them.

3. Have participants choose a partner and ask each person to select one attribute or action from the flipchart list and explain how he or she would incorporate it into his or her leadership style or circumstances.

4. Distribute the handout and ask the pairs to analyze the statements related to ethical leadership. (**Optional:** Announce that the first pair to answer all the questions correctly will win a prize.) The answers are 1ab; 2c; 3bc; 4a; 5abcd. Compliment the person who found them fastest.

5. Conclude with a brief discussion relating critical-thinking skills to leadership, in particular, the skills of discerning emerging patterns. Relate this leadership skill to current events, if possible.

VARIATION
The listing of attributes can be done for any number of additional programs, such as those with an emphasis on creativity, communication, sales, meeting effectiveness, et cetera.

DISCUSSION
Do you agree with Peter Drucker's assertion that leaders know how to ask questions—the right questions? If so, what constitutes "rightness," in terms of ethical behaviors? If you disagree, state the reason for your opposition.

QUOTATION
"The wise man doesn't give the right answers, he poses the right questions."
– Claude Levi-Strauss

POINTS OF INTEREST
Frank Navran, director of training for the Ethics Resource Center, located in Washington, D.C., cites five key motives that lead organizations to implement ethics training for *Successful Meetings* magazine: Legal, Moral, Perceptual, Pragmatic, and Change-oriented. Ask participants to critically analyze which of these motives is (or should be) motivating their own organizations.

Handout 4.1
Standing on Common Ground

Directions
Each numbered item below offers ideas about leader effectiveness. Determine which of the lettered statements following each numbered item describe the item correctly.

1. Ethical leaders don't hesitate to use books and television or movie screens to help them improve their skills, but they probably wouldn't turn to the radio for help.

   a. The first half alludes to visual tools; the second half does not.
   b. The first half cites double-lettered references; the second half does not.
   c. The first half has tools written in an alliterative manner; the second half does not.
   d. All of the above.
   e. None of the above.

2. To improve your persuasion skills as a leader, listen, report, declare, but don't compromise your values.

   a. The first half uses strong verbs; the second half does not.
   b. The first half is passive; the second half is not.
   c. The first half contains duo-syllabic exhortations; the second half does not.
   d. All of the above.
   e. None of the above.

3. As a leader, you should commit all your resources, communicate the pros and cons of your proposal, and convince using both anecdote and statistics, but you shouldn't deviate too far from your original intention.

   a. The first half is parallel; the second half is not.
   b. The first half has a series of recommendations; the second half does not.
   c. The first half is alliterative in its recommendation; the second half is not.
   d. All of the above.
   e. None of the above.

Handout 4.1: *Standing on Common Ground* (concluded)

4. As you set the parameters of your leadership project, you need to cite the alignment of resources and goals, the benefits that will accrue, and the constructs within which others will have to operate; but you don't need to generate an excessive number of possibilities.

    a. The first half is alpha-sequential; the second half is not.
    b. The first half contains infinitives; the second half does not.
    c. The first half contains a turnaround phrase; the second half does not.
    d. All of the above.
    e. None of the above.

5. Among other things, successful leaders know how to wow their followers and to bob with buoyancy when the waves of organizational opposition threaten to overwhelm them, but they don't know how to abandon their dreams very easily.

    a. The first half is longer than the second half.
    b. The first half contains a metaphor; the second half does not.
    c. The first half contains palindromic words; the second half does not.
    d. The first half contains alliteration; the second half does not.
    e. None of the above.

5. Ethical Leadership
False Prophets

Approximately 15 minutes

OVERVIEW
It's incumbent on all leaders, but especially those operating from an ethical base, to consider the weight their words carry. In this exercise, participants are asked to discuss the power that words have—both negative and positive power. Words that are not well chosen can even become a source of ridicule for the leader.

PURPOSE
- To better understand the effects a leader's words can have.
- To effect realization that leaders' words cannot always be equated with truth or reality.

GROUP SIZE
Any number of participants can participate.

ROOM ARRANGEMENT
No special arrangements required.

MATERIALS
- Handout 5.1, *"False Prophets"*
- **Optional:** Inexpensive pair of sunglasses

METHOD
1. Note that throughout history, virtually every leader who has accomplished his or her goal has encountered opposition of one sort or another. Frequently, that opposition comes from people in high positions who feel the goal is unattainable, the project not worth pursuing, and the purpose much too ambitious. These naysayers are often people with little or no vision. Ask participants for examples from history and from their own experiences that illustrate the opposition leaders initially meet.

2. Distribute the handout and tell the group they can work alone or in pairs to match the naysayer with his or her nonvisionary statement. (The answers are: 1C 2I 3G 4J 5F 6A 7H 8B 9D 10E.) Award a pair of sunglasses to the person who finishes first so that he or she will not be blinded by his or her own brilliance.

3. Bring closure to the exercise by asking participants to think of history's (or their organization's) leaders and the words that have inspired others to behave in responsible, ethical ways. Consider Winston Churchill's exhortation to the British people during World War II: "Never, never, never give up." Or John F. Kennedy's assertion to potential volunteers that the Peace Corps would be the toughest job they'd ever love.

VARIATION
Have participants discuss the myths (listed in the Points of Interest) with which they have had personal experience.

DISCUSSION
*   What expert opinions have been offered about a leadership project you're currently working on?

*   How much credence do you place in those opinions?

*   What things *are* likely to deter you from carrying out some leadership plan?

*   Whose words inspire you to continue?

QUOTATION
"The art of being wise is the art of knowing what to overlook."
– William James

POINTS OF INTEREST
Leaders who inaccurately prophesize may not be unethical. It's possible they simply lack good judgment. Sometimes, too, people perpetuate myths about ethics—myths that can seriously impact the ethical decisions others are trying to make. Author Nan DeMars lists these as the most common myths about ethical behavior:

*   ✓ "I have to do what I'm told—to keep my job!"

*   ✓ "I can trust my boss to always be fair."

*   ✓ "I can trust my company to always be fair."

*   ✓ "I really made a big mistake. I'm a bad person."

*   ✓ "What others do is none of my concern."

*   ✓ "I'm the only one who sees what's going on—and who cares."

*   ✓ "An action is either right or wrong."

*   ✓ "It's not my job to police my boss."

*   ✓ "I can't change this place."

- ✓ "A person cannot be talked into greater moral courage."
- ✓ "You are born with your morality."
- ✓ "Women have a more developed sense of ethics than men do."
- ✓ "People just naturally 'do the right thing' when presented with a moral dilemma."
- ✓ "Good employees don't do bad things. People act unethically because they are selfish, stupid, or bad."
- ✓ "Ethical management means ethical organizations."

Reprinted with permission from *You Want Me To Do What? When/Where & How to Draw the Line at Work* (Simon & Schuster) by Nan DeMars, Office Ethics Trainer/Consultant, President of Executary Services, a Seminar/Search/Office Ethics consultant firm in Minneapolis.

Handout 5.1

False Prophets

Directions

It's hard, but certainly not impossible, to remain stalwart in the face of expert opinion that views a leadership project as not worth pursuing. Sometimes, the opposition is rational, delivered in the best interests of the organization. At other times, however, the opposition may be based on unethical motives. But, we have to remember that the "experts" are not always right, as shown by the following predictions. Match the declaration to the misguided declarer. As you do, think about the weight these words may have carried.

_____ 1. "The atomic bomb will not go off. And I speak as an expert in explosives."

_____ 2. "What can be more palpably absurd than the prospect held out of locomotives traveling twice as fast as stagecoaches?"

_____ 3. "Babe Ruth made a big mistake when he gave up pitching."

4. "The telephone is an amazing invention, but who would ever want to use one of them?"

_____ 5. "People will soon get tired of staring at a plywood box every night."

_____ 6. "There is no reason for any individual to have a computer in their home."

_____ 7. "I was told that I wasn't big enough, maybe not fast enough and not strong enough."

_____ 8. "*Gone with the Wind* is going to be the biggest flop in the history of Hollywood. I'm just glad it'll be Clark Gable who's falling flat on his face and not me."

_____ 9. "Who the hell wants to hear actors talk?"

_____ 10. "While a calculator is now equipped with 18,000 vacuum tubes and weighs 30 tons, computers in the future may have only 1,000 vacuum tubes and only weigh one and a half tons."

Handout 5.1: *False Prophets* (concluded)

A. Ken Olson, former president of Digital Equipment Corporation

B. Gary Cooper

C. Admiral W. Leahy

D. Harry Warner, founder of Warner Brothers Studios, in 1927

E. 1949 issue of *Popular Mechanics*

F. Darryl F. Zanuck, former head of 20th Century Fox

G. Tris Speaker, Hall of Fame outfielder

H. Wayne Gretzky

I. *The Quarterly Review,* England, in March 1825

J. President Rutherford B. Hayes

Reproduced from *50 Reproducible Activities for Promoting Ethics Within the Organization*,
by Marlene Caroselli. HRD Press, 2015.

6. Ethical Leadership
Park Your Ethicar in the Harvard Yard

Approximately 45 minutes

OVERVIEW
A quarter of a century ago, Harvard undertook a study of why businesspeople behave unethically. With this exercise, participants list reasons for unethical behavior. They are then asked to prioritize their reasons as a small group and to compare their answers to those provided decades ago.

PURPOSE
To provoke thought and discussion regarding root causes of unethical behavior.

GROUP SIZE
Any size group. Participants will first work alone and then in small groups.

ROOM ARRANGEMENT
If possible, table groups for four or five participants.

MATERIALS
- Equipment for displaying PowerPoint slides
- Slide 6.1, *"Six Reasons"*
- **Optional:** Newspaper articles related to business ethics

METHOD
1. Begin with a brief discussion of current events related to business ethics. If possible, distribute the newspaper articles and allow a few moments for cursory review.

2. Next, ask participants, working alone, to list six possible reasons for such behavior.

3. Divide the audience into groups of four or five and ask them to share their answers and then to select the six most likely reasons. As a group, they will prioritize these reasons.

4. When they have finished, show Slide 6.1 and ask the small groups to compare their answers to a quarter-century-old survey of 1,227 readers of the *Harvard Business Review.*

5. Lead a discussion of the similarities and differences participants noted.

6. Ask each group to prepare a realistic plan of action that a leader could use to get at the root cause of unethical behavior and root it out.

VARIATION

Ask participants to devise a survey for use in their own organization. The survey should not only elicit reasons but should ask respondents to select possible ways of creating a more ethical culture.

DISCUSSION

- How much has really changed in terms of the rationale/excuses for unethical practices?

- What forces could lead a change for the better?

- To what extent can a leader influence others to change?

QUOTATION

"Time is a dressmaker specializing in alterations."
– Faith Baldwin

POINTS OF INTEREST

No one will ever argue that businesses are in business to make money. Yet money-making is not the only criterion for ethics-driven organizations. Consider Legg Mason, a holding company headquartered in Baltimore. They engage in securities brokerage, trading, investment management, and underwriting. Chip Mason, former chair, regarded honesty as the Number 1 principle on which his company operated. Second was an insistence that customers make a lot of money, and third, that brokers should not be greedy. In the words of authors Michael Mescon and Timothy Mescon, "Mason's personal code has become the professional code for the entire organization...."

Discuss with participants/leaders what their personal code is and how far it extends into their organizations.

Slide 6.1

Six Reasons Businesspeople Act Unethically

1. For personal financial reasons
2. As a result of society's values
3. Because of influence by peers
4. As a result of the industry's values
5. As a result of their companies' stated or unstated values
6. Because of influence by superiors

6.1

7. Ethical Leadership
You Don't Need Leaders to Tell People the Good News

Approximately 45 minutes (more, if the group is large)

OVERVIEW
You need leaders, according to Lee Iacocca, to tell people things they don't want to hear and then get them to do things they don't want to do. This exercise requires participants, working alone, to complete a comparison matrix. It then challenges them to think of a difficult-to-swallow message derived from the matrix and to strategize how that message can be made digestible.

PURPOSE
- To elicit thoughts regarding best ethical practices.
- To develop awareness of the gap between the ideal and the real.
- To outline a message that might close the ethical gap.

GROUP SIZE
The exercise will work with any size group. Participants first work alone and then make a short presentation to three others.

ROOM ARRANGEMENT
Flexible seating, if possible, so that participants can form small groups after working alone on the first part of the exercise.

MATERIALS
Handout 7.1, *"Comparison Matrix"*

PROCEDURE
1. Remind the group of management guru Tom Peters's advice: "If you have gone a whole week without being disobedient, you are not serving yourself or your company well." Discuss the possible meanings of "disobedient."

2. Note that one possible meaning is to express dissatisfaction with the organizational status quo, in an effort to promote continuous improvement.

3. Distribute the handout and ask participants to fill it out. (**Note:** If you spot some people struggling with the best practices for the first column, quietly suggest they work with another person. Avoid possible embarrassment with a comment such as, "That's the part I had the most trouble with myself. I had to call a colleague for help. Do you mind if I have you and _____ work together on this?")

4. Once the handout is complete, ask participants, still working alone, to outline a brief "speech" they would make to their manager or other high-level organizational leader. The speech would explain the need to remove a specific barrier and would suggest ways the removal could be implemented. The speech should last 5 minutes, at the very most.

5. Next, have participants form groups of four. Each person in the subgroup will deliver his or her speech and will receive feedback from the others in the group.

6. Bring closure to the exercise by asking what it would take for these speeches to actually be delivered.

VARIATION
This exercise could easily be adapted for:

•   Presentation programs (for which participants would actually deliver the speech)

•   Leadership programs (for which participants would develop a proposal and work to have it approved and then implemented)

•   Communications programs (for which participants would employ specific persuasion tools, such as those described in the Points of Interest)

DISCUSSION
•   In what ways have you "defied" the status quo in recent months?
•   One definition of a "leader" is the person who takes others where they would not have gone without him or her. To what places do people in your organization need to "travel"?
•   How else could you use a gap analysis to effect improvement in your organization?

QUOTATION
"All that really matters is devotion to something bigger than ourselves."
– Teilhard de Chardin

POINTS OF INTEREST

Keep in mind these D-words as you work to persuade others to adapt your recommendations:

- **Drama**—Heighten the emotional appeal of your presentation by adding a bit of drama to it. The excitement could appear in your voice, in your body language, or in the content of your remarks. A surprising statistic is just one of the ways you could add depth and texture to your message.

- **Developments**—Relating current events (both inside and outside the organization) to the need for the change you are proposing is an effective means of persuasion. You can use the events to validate the success-likelihood of your idea or to suggest a given outcome could be avoided if your plan were implemented.

- **Deprecation (self only)**—At the 2002 Academy Awards presentation, Woody Allen told the audience that he offered the names of fourteen other filmmakers who would be even better representatives of New York City than he himself. Then he told them that the caller admitted they had already tried the others and none of them were available. Such humor almost always serves to develop a rapport with an audience. Translated into a business setting, participants might say something like this prior to making their proposal to their manager: *"I envy the experience you have in this industry. Even though I'm relatively new, I think I've come up with a way we could improve the communication flow in our office."*

Handout 7.1
Comparison Matrix

Directions

Begin by listing, as specifically as possible, five of the best practices in which leaders should engage, in your opinion. In the second column, do a reality check: indicate the extent to which one or more leaders in your organization are executing each of these practices. Finally, specify the barriers that would have to be removed if the gap between the ideal and the real were to be closed.

Best Leadership Practices	*Current Practices*	*Barriers*
1.		
2.		
3.		
4.		
5.		

8. Ethical Leadership
Machiavellian, Manipulative, or Masterful?

Approximately 30 minutes

OVERVIEW
This exercise begins with a quiz that, ideally, helps participants realize that Machiavellian behavior, and even manipulative behavior, can actually benefit all parties involved. They then work in pairs to discuss what they would have done in two real-world situations.

PURPOSE
- To relate Machiavellian principles to positive business practices.
- To stimulate discussion of ethically appropriate behavior.

GROUP SIZE
Any number of participants can engage in this exercise, which calls initially for individual work and then paired discussions.

ROOM ARRANGEMENT
No special configurations required.

MATERIALS
- Handout 8.1, *"Historical Applications"*
- Handout 8.2, *"How Machiavellian Are You?"*
- Handout 8.3, *"What Would You Do?"*

METHOD
1. Conduct a short discussion regarding the importance of open-mindedness in those who would lead. (You may choose to cite the example of Roger Boisjolie, a junior engineer, who tried repeatedly, but unsuccessfully, to warn his superiors of a problem with the O-ring in the Challenger shuttle.)

2. Explain that the handout you are distributing (Handout 8.1, "Historical Applications") will afford them an opportunity to learn if they can look beyond certain negative connotations in order to find the value in a given set of circumstances.

3. After they complete the test, distribute Handout 8.2 ("How Machiavellian Are You?") and allow a few minutes for participants to read the interpretation of it. Discuss the fact that we often recoil from certain words (or people or situations) without fully exploring the possible value inherent in those contexts.

4. Next, distribute Handout 8.3 and ask participants to work in pairs to complete it.

5. Debrief with an exchange that acknowledges that it may be absolutely ethical for a leader to engage in behavior that is "Machiavellian" (in the broadest sense of the word) and even in behavior that is manipulative.

VARIATION

Icebreaker: Divide participants into small groups and ask them to share labels that have been bestowed upon them over the years (for example, "worrywart"). Then have each person explain the potential merit in that word—citing, perhaps, a time when they were very grateful that they *did* worry over the details someone else might have ignored.

DISCUSSION

*   What other words do people recoil from?
*   What merit could lie behind some of these words?
*   How open are the lines of communication and consideration in your own organization?

QUOTATION

"We are all of us all the time coming together and falling apart. The point is we are not rocks. Who wants to be one anyway, impermeable, unchanging, our history already played out...."

– John Rosenthal

POINTS OF INTEREST

An article by marketing consultant and speaker Terry Mandel encourages us to revisit the meaning of the word *competition*. He suggests that by moving from an us-versus-them mind-set and toward the original meaning of the word—"striving together"—we can regard competitors as mirrors reflecting a direction in which we should be moving.

Handout 8.1
Historical Applications

Directions
Read the following statements and answer **Agree** or **Disagree,** depending on the extent to which you agree with the truth of the statement. Think of the degree to which the statement matches your way of thinking. If you both agree and disagree with a given statement, try to determine which choice you'd agree with just slightly more than the other choice. Instead of a 50/50 response, then, you would consider the statement as a choice between 51/49 percent; you would favor one response slightly more than the other. (There are no trick questions here. Simply tell if you agree or disagree with the statements.)

Place a check ☑ in the appropriate box to the right of each statement.

		Agree	Disagree
1.	We should be adaptable when unforeseen events occur.	❏	❏
2.	One change always leaves indentations on which to build another change.	❏	❏
3.	In the beginning, problems are easy to cure but hard to diagnose; with the passage of time, having gone unrecognized and unattended, they become easy to diagnose, but hard to cure.	❏	❏
4.	A workplace accustomed to freedom is more easily managed by its own employees than by any other arrangement.	❏	❏
5.	A wise influencer must always tread the path of great men and women and should imitate those who have excelled.	❏	❏
6.	People who least rely on luck alone will be the most successful.	❏	❏
7.	Success is a combination of opportunity and ability.	❏	❏
8.	Most people have no faith in new things until they have been proved by experiences.	❏	❏
9.	If you have to beg others to fulfill a mission, you are destined to fail.	❏	❏

Handout 8.1: *Historical Applications* (concluded)

	Agree	Disagree
10. If you are respected, you will be secure, honored, and successful.	❏	❏
11. Things that come easily are hard to maintain. Things that are hard won are easier to maintain.	❏	❏
12. A leader who thinks more about his/her own interests than about yours, who seeks his/her own advantage for everything he/she does, will never be a good leader, for others will never be able to trust him/her.	❏	❏
13. In order to keep employees loyal, managers must honor them by sharing both distinctions and duties.	❏	❏

Reproduced from *50 Reproducible Activities for Promoting Ethics Within the Organization*, by Marlene Caroselli. HRD Press, 2015.

Handout 8.2
How Machiavellian Are You?

Interpretation

Because there are 13 items, if you had 7 or more in one category, then that is your "majority" category. Which category, **Agree** or **Disagree,** is your majority category? _____

Now let's see how open you are to influences that do not represent typical sources of knowledge acquisition. In all likelihood, you agreed with at least 7 of the statements. Would it "shock" you to learn that these 13 paraphrased statements are taken from *The Prince* by Niccolo Macchiavelli? Written 500 years ago, the book has become synonymous with words like "duplicity" and "deceit." And yet, much of what it endorses makes sense for today's leader, manager, and/or influencer.

Does a majority of **Agree** answers mean you are Machiavellian, in the most negative sense of the word? No, not at all. It means simply that no one thing is 100 percent "right" or 100 percent "wrong." Even in *The Prince* there is wisdom from which we can profit. But … if you are not open, you won't be able to spot the worth; your stamp of "worthless" will prevent you from seeing worth in hard realities. If you take no risks into the unpopular or unknown, you will not be able to optimize or reify possibilities that lie hidden in the here and now.

Remember that selling a particular service, product, or proposal to others depends on your understanding of the current reality and your ability to remain mentally flexible or open to new ideas. Not until you have achieved these mental states can you create the new reality. It's often true that "if you build it, they will come," but if you don't hear or see the possibilities calling to you, you will never be able to reify them.

Reproduced from *50 Reproducible Activities for Promoting Ethics Within the Organization*, by Marlene Caroselli. HRD Press, 2015.

Handout 8.3
What Would You Do?

Directions
In the blank space beneath each scenario, tell what course of action you would have taken and why. Be prepared to answer the questions that follow each real-life case study, too.

1. Brenda believed she had to work harder than most men to make it in her company, a major defense contractor. She worked hard, perhaps harder than she had to, and let her work speak for itself. She was often described as a straight-shooting, no-nonsense manager whose loyalty to the firm and whose honesty were impeccable. She made progress but didn't reach the levels she had set as goals for herself by a certain time. She was discussing the situation one day with Judy, another manager who was moving very rapidly along her own career path. In an effort to be helpful, Judy suggested if Brenda were willing to use her "feminine wiles," she could move ahead more rapidly.

    If you were Brenda, what would you have done? _____

    _____

    _____

    _____

    _____

    (1) Are there ethical issues involved in using one's feminine or masculine "wiles"? If so, what are they?

    (2) What are the criteria by which people move rapidly ahead in a corporate setting?

    (3) Relate this statement by Don Petersen, former head of Ford Motor Company—*"Results depend on relationships"*—to this situation.

Handout 8.3: *What Would You Do?* (concluded)

2. Mark was known throughout the department as being a "stand-up kind of guy"—respected by everyone for his honesty, trustworthiness, and dependability. Jerry Fletcher, his boss, asked to see him one day and explained that he had heard "rumblings" about the sexist behavior of a particular employee—behavior that was not visible whenever Jerry was in the vicinity. Despite Jerry's frequently stated policy about sexual harassment, Jerry suspected the lack of formal complaint didn't mean there was no problem. He worried that one day, someone would simply decide enough was enough and would file a lawsuit. Consequently, he asked Mark to spy on the employee and to report back to him.

If you were Mark, what would you have done? _____

_____

_____

_____

_____

(1) What possible reasons could explain why there might be no formal complaints in a situation like this?

(2) What does the law state regarding behaviors that constitute sexual harassment?

(3) On what factors should Mark base his decision to do or not do what his boss is asking?

Reproduced from *50 Reproducible Activities for Promoting Ethics Within the Organization*, by Marlene Caroselli. HRD Press, 2015.

9. Ethical Leadership
Be-Guile

Approximately 25 minutes

OVERVIEW

Participants are asked to think like leaders in this exercise and to consider changes they believe are needed in their organizations. They provide three ideas in each of three categories and then draft a letter to their manager proposing the one change they believe is most critical.

PURPOSE

- To encourage thinking about necessary organizational changes.
- To encourage action that might result in the change actually taking place.

GROUP SIZE

Any size group can work on this exercise. Participants will first work alone and then with two others.

ROOM ARRANGEMENT

Any classroom set-up will work for this exercise.

MATERIALS

- Handout 9.1, *"Let It Be"*
- Circular adhesive dots
- **Optional:** Token prizes, such as pens, for members of the winning triad

PROCEDURE

Open by asking for a show of hands in response to these questions:

1. How many of you enjoy change? How many of you think the average employee fears change? How many of you create change?

2. Ask a participant who raised his or her hand for all three questions to come forward and serve as a moderator to questions participants might have about change. If no questions are being asked, you might ask for answers to the three questions asked earlier. Or, ask additional ones such as, "What are some changes you feel are necessary in your department?" "In your organization?" "Why are these changes not taking place?"

3. Once you feel participants are thinking along the lines of needed change, distribute the handout and allow 5 to 10 minutes for its completion.

4. Ask participants to review what they've written and to select the one change-item they feel should be implemented the most.

5. Have participants work with two others. Have the triad discuss their choices and then have them vote on the one change-item (among the three) that the triad feels is most critical.

6. Have the triads work together to compose a letter that, ideally, would convince a member of senior management to institute the necessary change. Ask them to write as legibly as possible and not to put their names (or their managers' names) on the letters.

7. Post the letters around the room.

8. Distribute one adhesive dot to each participant with the instruction to vote for the letter they feel would most convince management to take action. (They will vote by affixing their dot to the letter of their choice.)

9. Award prizes or at least applaud the triad with the winning letter. Read it aloud, perhaps more than once, and debrief by asking participants what specific elements they found compelling.

10. Conclude with a reference to Ken Blanchard's quotation (below).

VARIATION
Invite a member of senior management to read the posted letters, instead of having participants do so. Have the manager decide which is the one he or she would be most likely to take action on. Ask for input regarding the content/context that encouraged that action.

DISCUSSION
- What prevents people from taking action on things that clearly need to be improved?
- Under what conditions are you most inspired or motivated to get things done?
- Does guilt ever play a role in encouraging action?

QUOTATION
"The key to leadership today is influence, not authority."
– Ken Blanchard

POINTS OF INTEREST

In some ways, the environment is much like the weather: everyone talks about it but not everyone does something about it. Not so for SET Laboratories, Inc., of Mulino, Oregon. When the company ships software, they depend on real popcorn instead of fake peanuts—the polystyrene kind. Not only is the popcorn better for the environment, it even costs less—by 60 percent.

Handout 9.1
Let It Be

Directions
Think about your own team, work unit, department, or even your own organization or industry.

- What are some changes that ought to be made? List three of these changes in the first column below.

- Next, consider some changes that "have got" to be implemented, even though you may not have a part in that implementation, and/or you don't know when that implementation might occur. List three of these changes in the second column.

- Finally, regard changes that you can put in place yourself. List three of these changes that would be within your power to institute. These should be changes that you feel strongly about—so strongly that you can actually make a commitment to implementing them. In the third column, list three things that are going to be different from now on.

Oughtta Be	Gotta Be	Gonna Be

10. Ethical Leadership
More P-O-W-E-R to You

Approximately 45 minutes

OVERVIEW
Words beginning with each of the letters that spell *power* are listed for discussion purposes. Participants first make individual choices and then attempt to reach group consensus. The same process is then used as participants react to statements about leadership.

PURPOSE
- To spark ideas about the correlations between power and leadership.
- To challenge participants to reach consensus about leadership statements.

GROUP SIZE
Any number of participants can work on this exercise, which has two parts. In each part, participants first work alone and then as part of a group.

ROOM ARRANGEMENT
Ideally, seating is flexible so that participants can move seats to form subgroups twice during the exercise.

MATERIALS
- Flipchart and marking pens
- Handout 10.1, *"Leading a Group"*

PROCEDURE
1. Write the letters P–O–W–E–R on the flipchart.

2. Ask participants, working alone, to come up with three words, beginning with the letter "p," that relate to either leadership and/or to ethics. Next, they will think of three words starting with the letter "o" that also relate to leadership and/or to ethics. They will continue in this manner with the letters "w," "e," and "r."

3. After approximately 10 minutes, ask participants to determine which of all those words is the most important for a person practicing ethical leadership. They should place a checkmark in front of that word on their papers.

4. Ask the class to form groups of four or five. Each person will tell his or her word and then the group will attempt to reach consensus on the one word that is most relevant or critical to the practice of ethical leadership.

5. Distribute the handout and ask participants to write their Agree or Disagree answers on the left-hand column only.

6. Form different groups of four or five this time. Task the groups with achieving consensus on the statements regarding leadership.

7. Debrief by asking a spokesperson from each group to briefly describe their process. After each person finishes, ask pertinent questions about the way power was used (if it was at all) as the groups worked to reach full agreement.

VARIATION

Appoint an observer for each group as they work to achieve consensus. Have the observers look specifically for participants who demonstrate leadership by suggesting compromise positions that might enable the group to reach accord about the statements. For example, the observer would be looking for someone who suggests altering the wording. (The directions do not prohibit such action.) Afterwards, ask the observers to meet for a few moments outside the room and to appoint one spokesperson who will make general comments about a leader's ability to achieve agreement, as reflected in this microcosmic assignment.

DISCUSSION

*   Beyond the obvious abuse-of-power answer, why does the word "power" carry such negative connotations?

*   To what extent do you feel leaders should enjoy exercising power?

*   How would you define "power"?

QUOTATION
"Tell the truth, but make the truth fascinating."
– David Ogilvy

POINTS OF INTEREST
As reported in *The Economist*, Harvard began offering courses in business ethics back in 1915. Today, it is rare for business programs not to include such courses. One business school sends MBA students to a monastery for a few weeks of soul-searching. Consider ways organizations can encourage such searches without having employees leave the premises.

Handout 10.1
Leading a Group

Directions
First read each statement and tell if you agree or disagree with it. Circle the letter "A" or "D" in the left-hand column to indicate how you feel about each statement. Then, work with four or five others, attempt to reach consensus on each of the statements, and circle the corresponding letter in the right-hand column.

Individual				*Group*	
A	D	1.	The purpose of leadership is to develop other leaders.	A	D
A	D	2.	As an employee of my organization, I feel my leadership opportunities are limited.	A	D
A	D	3.	It's hard to exercise leadership over others because most employees are simply interested in earning their salary, not in contributing to the organization.	A	D
A	D	4.	It's hard to exert leadership because the people above us don't listen to us.	A	D
A	D	5.	People who use power well tend to have big egos.	A	D
A	D	6.	To be an effective leader, you must have some drive toward self-aggrandizement.	A	D
A	D	7.	People who strive to be leaders are primarily interested in advancing their own careers.	A	D
A	D	8.	Leaders are born, not made.	A	D
A	D	9.	"Change agent" is a phrase that could be substituted for "leader."	A	D
A	D	10.	A good leader must be a good communicator.	A	D

Reproduced from *50 Reproducible Activities for Promoting Ethics Within the Organization*, by Marlene Caroselli. HRD Press, 2015.

Part B:
Ethical Corporate Citizenship
***Introduction*: Thomas J. Mitrano**

When I was in law school, we used to have heated debates about whether corporations should—or even could—be held to the same standards as human citizens are. Today, thinking back to those days, I'm reminded of the intense and risky fight Ansel Adams, Imogen Cunningham, Edward Weston, and others waged over whether photography could be considered an art form.

Today, such debates seem almost quaint. Of course photography is an art form. Of course corporations are subject to standards of fairness and legality like flesh-and-blood citizens.

Still, for many years, the "citizenship" of corporations was significant mostly for tax, accounting, and business operations matters. Although these concerns continue, the growing focus on the day-to-day implications of citizenship for entities created by law, not DNA, raises complex issues, both profound and profane, for all of us who manage, enter into relationships with, or are otherwise affected by our fellow corporate citizens.

In many respects, legislation and the courts provide answers to many basic questions raised by the existence of rights and privileges of corporations. For years, the common law has denied wrongdoing corporate directors, shareholders, and owner-managers the synthetic protection of the "corporate veil." The venerable Employee Retirement Income Security Act ("ERISA") and its regulations impose extensive sets of rules aimed at imposing a fairness standard when companies create retirement programs for their staff. Employment and hiring practices legislation, civil rights laws, gender equity, and sexual-preferences cases—all are aimed at bringing a legal abstraction, the "corporation," down to earth by defining the duties and social mores with which corporations must comply in relationships with individuals.

The Foreign Corrupt Practices Act has tackled the ethically and culturally complex area of standards for business practices for our corporate citizens all over the world. Criminal actions against vast international corporations and their auditors and attorneys seek to overlay a very real set of criminal consequences onto the decision-making and operations of even the largest organizations.

But, the exploration of the meaning of citizenship for corporations does not stop with the legal, judicial, legislative, regulatory, or criminal infrastructure of our society. In fact, for most of us, day-to-day, there are many more practical issues that concern us. How does a good corporate citizen "write and circulate e-mail"?

Can a corporate employer eavesdrop on staff members' communications with impunity? Should corporate citizens be under a greater duty to balance business with humanity's environmental needs than noncorporate citizens? What exactly are the burdens of being bigger than any other kid on the block (by virtue of being able to concentrate vast resources)?

Human scale issues like privacy, patriotism, initiative, reputation, candor, ego, anger, and loss are being examined anew today as we consider implications at the corporate citizen level.

The well-equipped employee, manager, and person in the street today need a new competence and literacy in, as well as a new attitude toward, issues like these.

The following chapter's objective is to develop that competence and introduce that literacy. By thoughtfully considering the issues and working through the exercises, the involved reader will assume a competence-based, proactive position able to deal with, manage, and mutually benefit from relationships with fellow corporate citizens.

Submitted by: Thomas J. Mitrano
                  TomM@AMPartners.com

Thomas J. Mitrano, Esq., is General Counsel and Principal at AM Partners, Inc., an internationally recognized architecture, interiors, planning, and graphics firm located in Honolulu, Hawaii. A resident of Hawaii since 1982, Mr. Mitrano is a graduate of the University of Toronto (1968) and Harvard Law School (1972). He is admitted to practice law in Hawaii, California, and before several federal courts. Mr. Mitrano has practiced at law offices in New York, Tokyo, Los Angeles, and Carmel, California. He has taught corporate, business, and commercial law courses.

Mr. Mitrano is also a consultant and business professional with development, managerial, operational, and planning expertise applied in the high-tech, architecture, and visitor industries, in banking, and in the nonprofit sector. He is an accomplished writer, speaker, and legislative lobbyist, with a high-level, nonnative speaker's competency in reading, writing, and speaking Mandarin Chinese.

11. Ethical Corporate Citizenship
Verbally Abusive Behavior

60 to 90 minutes

OVERVIEW
Participants are encouraged to think about the ethical ramifications of verbally abusive behavior/situations in the work environment.

PURPOSE
To make participants aware of how verbally abusive behaviors affect job performance, organizational perspectives, and interpersonal relationships.

GROUP SIZE
Ideal group size is 18 to 20 participants.

ROOM ARRANGEMENT
Select a room large enough for a subgroup to break out. Set up the main work area in a "U" shape, allowing room for the facilitator to enter the "U" and be in the middle of the discussions.

MATERIALS
- Equipment for displaying PowerPoint slides
- Slides 11.1 through 11.7 showing questions
- Tape for hanging the flipchart sheets on the wall
- Magic markers
- Post-it® notes (3 x 3 size), in bright colors if possible
- Flipchart with the activity headings written at the top of each page. (As the pages are completed, they should be hung on the wall for viewing.)

Headings and set-up for flipchart sheets:

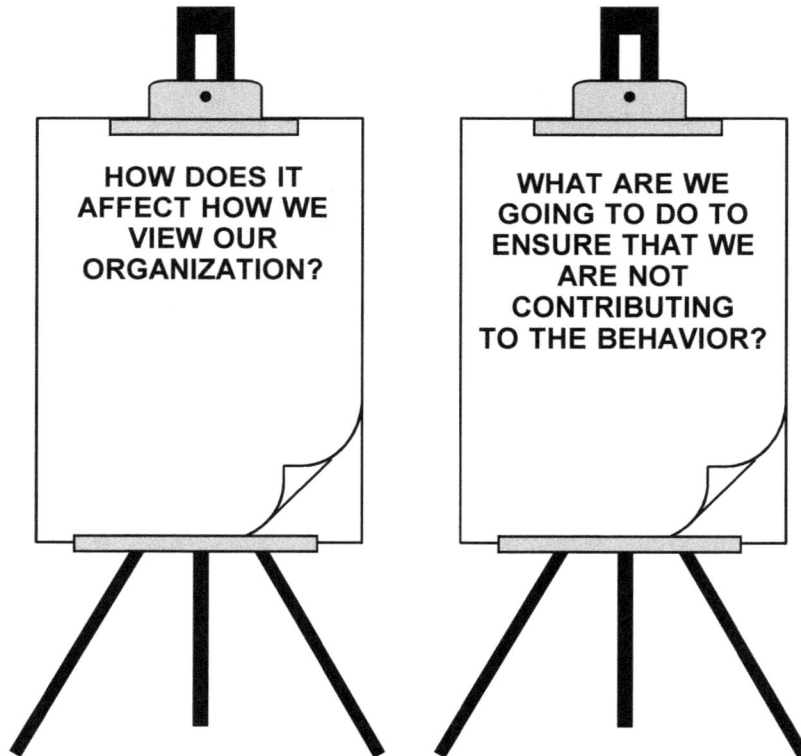

GROUND RULES

HOW DID THIS MAKE YOU FEEL?

How did this experience affect...

YOUR WORK	YOUR HOME LIFE

WHAT DOES THIS COMMUNICATE TO THOSE WORKING IN THE ORGANIZATION?

HOW DOES IT AFFECT HOW WE VIEW OUR ORGANIZATION?

WHAT ARE WE GOING TO DO TO ENSURE THAT WE ARE NOT CONTRIBUTING TO THE BEHAVIOR?

PROCEDURE

1. Spend the first 5 minutes establishing ground rules with participants. These rules encourage a more open environment, permitting individuals to share without feeling they are overstepping bounds. The rules might deal with confidentiality, for example: *"What is shared in the room stays in the room"* and *"No names—company or people."*

2. Show Slide 11.1 posting the question, *"How many of you have witnessed verbally abusive situations in your workplace?"* Ask participants to pair up to share their experiences with one another for 5 to 10 minutes.

3. Next, facilitate a discussion for approximately 10 minutes by inviting the group as a whole to share experiences. Use the question on Slide 11.2 (*"How many of you have personally experienced verbal abuse?"*) to stimulate the discussion. **Note:** Be prepared for emotions to surface during this part of the exercise. Intercede if you observe any participant becoming emotional; say something like: *"Before you finish, let me share with you an experience of my own"* to allow the participant to compose him- or herself. Of course, you could also ask, *"Would you prefer to tell us the rest of this terrible story later?"*

4. Proceed to the next question on Slide 11.3, *"How did this make you feel?"* Have a flipchart sheet ready with the same heading at the top. This part of the exercise calls for participants to answer the question individually and silently. Instruct them to write their feelings on the Post-it® notes (one comment per sheet). Invite participants to share what they've written and then to hang the Post-it® notes on the flipchart sheet. Facilitate any discussion that takes place at this time.

5. Show Slide 11.4 and ask the question, *"How did this affect your work?"* The flipchart page will be set up as a "T" chart with "Your Home Life" covered up at this time. This part of the exercise has participants working alone. Instruct them to write their comments on the Post-it® notes (one per sheet). After a few minutes, invite the participants to share what they've written and then to hang the Post-it® notes on the flipchart sheet. Facilitate any discussion that takes place at this time.

6. Show Slide 11.5 and ask the question, *"How did this affect your home life?"* Uncover the right side of the "T" chart on the flipchart titled, **Your Home Life.** This portion of the exercise, once again, is completed individually. Instruct the participants to write their comments on the Post-it® notes (one per sheet). Encourage discussion among participants of what they've written and then invite them to hang the Post-it® notes on the flipchart sheet.

7. As you display Slide 11.6, ask the question, *"When this behavior is allowed to continue, what does this communicate to those working in the organization?"* Ask participants to pair up and share with one another what they feel is communicated and why. Instruct them next to write their comments on the Post-it® notes (one per sheet). Facilitate any discussion that arises at this time.

8. Continue with the question on Slide 11.7, *"When this behavior is allowed to continue, how does it affect how we view our organization?"* Ask participants to form pairs and share with one another specifically how such behavior and the allowance of it affects their view of the organization. Instruct them to write their comments on the Post-it® notes (one per sheet). Invite participants to share their thoughts and then to hang the Post-it® notes on the flipchart sheet. Facilitate any discussion that takes place at this time.

9. Conclude by asking the participants, *"What have you learned through this exercise?"* Facilitate the discussion and bring in key points of interest from the flipchart sheets hanging on the wall. Then ask the question, *"With what we have learned today about how abusive behaviors affect us at work and at home, what are we going to do to ensure that we are not contributing to this behavior?"* Facilitate an open discussion and describe comments on a flipchart sheet.

DISCUSSION
- Does your organization have a policy regarding violence in the workplace? If so, what does it say about verbally abusive behavior?
- If not, what should it say about such behavior?

QUOTATIONS
"Be the change you want to see in others."

– Gundi

"Everything I do and say with anyone makes a difference."

– Gita Bellin

"Everyone and everything around you is your teacher."

– Ken Keyes, Jr.

POINTS OF INTEREST
It doesn't take much imagination to realize that verbally abusive behavior can easily move from a verbal altercation to physical blows. The statistics concerning violence in the workplace are truly alarming.

The National Institute for Occupational Safety and Health (NIOSH) views homicide within the work environment as a "significant" problem. Fifteen percent of the 6,200 deaths that occur in the workplace each year are homicides, making such fatalities the second leading cause of death in the workplace. For women, it's the number one cause of death in the workplace.

Further, the National Safe Workplace Institute (NSWPI) reports that nearly 25 percent of all employees report having been threatened, harassed, or actually attacked on the job in recent years.

Two million employees report physical attacks. The cost of these attacks, in lost work and legal expenses alone, is nearing $40 billion. The actual cost may be higher: 55 percent of victims indicate they failed to report incidents to police.

Submitted by: Eve Strella and Gwen Martone
                     Illuminate of Rochester, Inc.
                     15 Stuyvesant Road
                     Suite 100
                     Pittsford, New York 14534
                     Phone and fax: 585-385-9699
                     E-mail: estrella@thexlr8team.com
                     Web site: www.lightyourpath.com

Illuminate of Rochester, Inc., is a coaching, consulting, training, and team development organization whose focus is to assist individuals and organizations in transition through issues of change, layoffs, mergers, abusive management and co-worker behavior, and fear in the workplace. Co-CEOs Eve Strella and Gwen Martone have merged their expertise as an industrial engineer and a clinical therapist with a combined 32 years of hands-on experience in the area of human solutions.

Slide 11.1

> How many of you have witnessed verbally abusive situations in your workplace?
>
> 11.1

Slide 11.2

> How many of you have personally experienced verbal abuse?
>
> 11.2

Slide 11.3

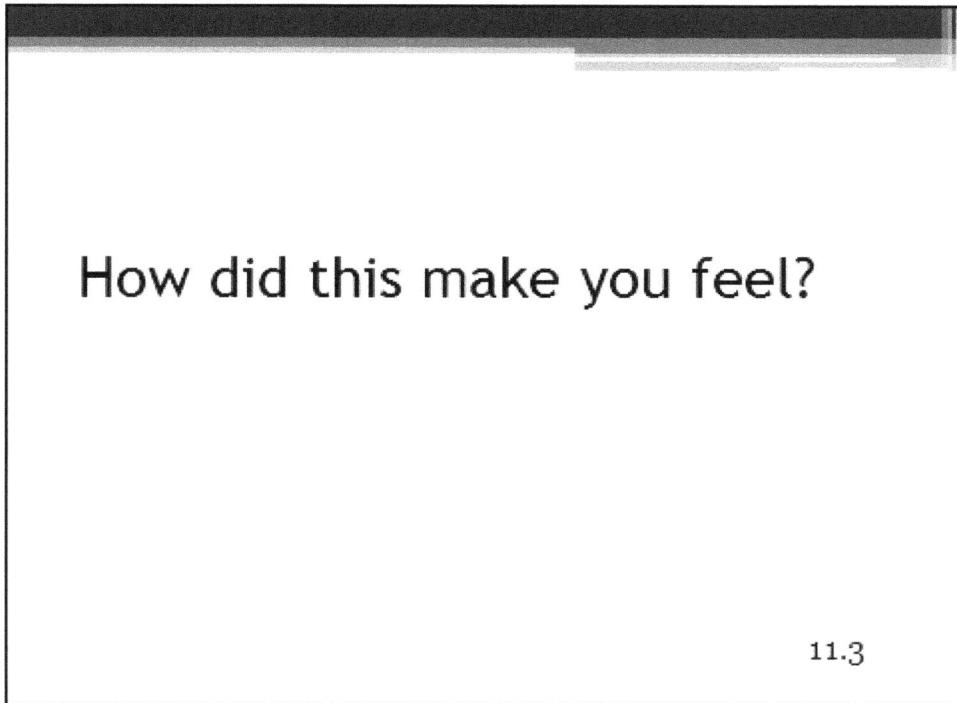

How did this make you feel?

11.3

Slide 11.4

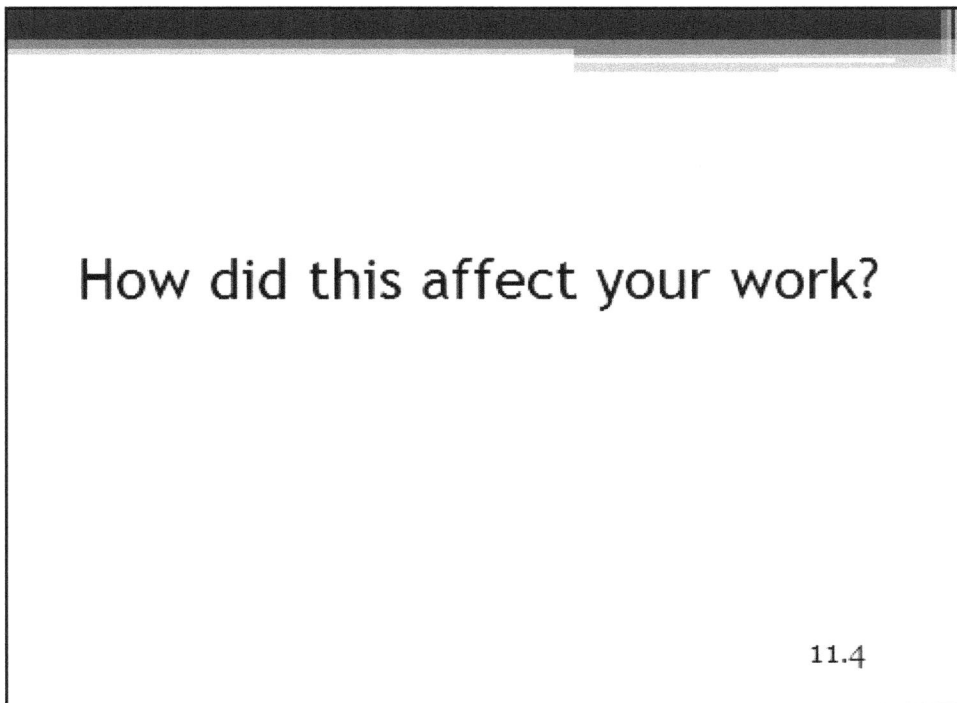

How did this affect your work?

11.4

Slide 11.5

> How did this affect your
> home life?
>
> 11.5

Slide 11.6

> When this behavior is allowed
> to continue, what does this
> communicate to those working
> in the organization?
>
> 11.6

Slide 11.7

When this behavior is allowed to continue, how does it affect how we view our organization?

11.7

12. Ethical Corporate Citizenship
E-Mail Ethics

Approximately 15 minutes

OVERVIEW
Participants are encouraged to think about the ethical consequences of seemingly innocent acts, such as circulating humorous Internet lists to co-workers.

PURPOSE
To make participants aware of personal and organizational liabilities associated with misuse of the Internet.

GROUP SIZE
Any size group, divided into subgroups of three or four.

ROOM ARRANGEMENT:
If possible, table groups for four participants.

MATERIALS
- Equipment for displaying PowerPoint slides
- Slide 12.1, *"Internet and Productivity"*
- Handout 12.1, *"What's Your EQ (Electronic Quotient)?"*

PROCEDURE
1. Begin by asking if anyone has recently received any good lists at work. These would be funny composites of responses to questions such as, "How Can You Tell You're Getting Old?" or "Ways to Get Back at the Boss" or "25 Things You Should Never Tell Your Spouse" or "Why Jesus May Have Been Mexican." Allow a minute or two for sharing.

2. Then show the questions on Slide 12.1, *"Internet and Productivity."* Ask participants to pair up and discuss one or two of the questions for about 5 minutes.

3. Distribute Handout 12.1. Ask participants to answer the questions and then lead a brief discussion based on the answers: 1. B ("Email: Tool or Torment?" in *Solutions*, Summer 2001, page 15); 2. C ("Secrets & Lies," by Bruce Schneier, *Upside*, October 2000, page 266); 3. D ("Plain and Simple," by Tom MacDonald, *Successful Meetings*, April 2000, page 32); 4. E ("The rules of E-etiquette," by Dana May Casperson, *Incentive*, October 2000, page 140); 5. A.

4. Conclude by incorporating the Points of Interest in your reminder that electronic surfing, sending, and receiving of material not related to work reduces productivity. Further, they may violate internal policy and could cost employees their jobs.

VARIATION
Icebreaker: Begin the class by distributing the handout. Ask participants to find others who had the same answers they did. (They can form dyads, triads, or small groups. Those who cannot find anyone with an identical set of answers can form a "group" of their own.) Ask which group had answers B, C, D, E, A. Ask them to stand for an ovation from the other participants. Then probe: "Were these lucky guesses or do some of you have some experience with e-mail ethics? If so, can you share that with us now?"

DISCUSSION
*   What's the most efficient way to write a policy regarding e-mail usage?
*   What's the best way of enforcing such a policy?
*   Should such policies have "zero tolerance"?
*   Do employers have the right to invade employees' electronic privacy?

QUOTATION
"In the event of a workplace lawsuit, employees' home computers may be reviewed along with the company's computers."
                              – Nancy Flynn, author *The ePolicy Handbook*

POINTS OF INTEREST
*   An e-mail circulated by male employees ("25 reasons why beer is better than women") cost a major corporation $2.2 million to settle a sexual harassment lawsuit.

*   Don't think that just because you've deleted a message you wish you hadn't received, your computer actually deletes it. The message stays on your hard drive and can be retrieved fairly easily.

Slide 12.1

Internet and Productivity

1. Does your company have an Internet/email policy? If so, what are its main points? If not, what do you think it should include?

2. How much time do you spend each week sending/ receiving information that is not directly related to your job?

3. How much time do you think is spent by others in your department?

4. Calculate the cost, on an annual basis, of this time.

5. How much regulation is too much regulation?

6. How often should e-files be purged?

12.1

Handout 12.1
What's Your EQ?

1. How much time does the average executive spend using e-mail?
   A. 20 minutes per day
   B. 2 hours per day
   C. 20 hours per week
   D. 200 hours per year
   E. None of the above.

2. How many U.S. corporations have personal databases (containing our financial, medical, and lifestyle details)?
   A. 200
   B. 2000
   C. 20,000
   D. 200,000
   E. None of the above.

3. What percentage of employees, managers, and executives are so flooded with information they can't find what they need to make a decision?
   A. 17%
   B. 37%
   C. 57%
   D. 70%
   E. 87%

4. Which of these recommendations reflects responsible e-mail usage?
   A. Responding within 24 hours, no matter who sent the e-mail.
   B. Eliminating reference of the sender's original message to save time for both of you.
   C. Omitting your phone number and address.
   D. All of the above.
   E. None of the above.

5. "Antiperspirants cause breast cancer." If you wanted to verify the truth of an e-rumor such as this, you could visit this web site:

   nonprofit.net/-hoax/default.htm.

   A. True
   B. False

Reproduced from *50 Reproducible Activities for Promoting Ethics Within the Organization*, by Marlene Caroselli. HRD Press, 2015.

13. Ethical Corporate Citizenship
To Be or Not to Be…Civil

Approximately 25 minutes

OVERVIEW

This exercise helps participants explore the line (not always a fine one) between the letter of the law and the spirit of the law. It takes a real-world scenario and asks participants to compare it to similar situations they've experienced.

PURPOSE

To encourage thought and discussion regarding instances when it may be appropriate to break, bend, or ignore the rules that govern a corporate entity.

GROUP SIZE

Any size group, divided into subgroups of four or five.

ROOM ARRANGEMENT

If possible, table groups for four or five participants.

MATERIALS

* Equipment for displaying PowerPoint slides
* Slide 13.1, *"Discussion Questions"*

METHOD

1. Share with the class this true story, as reported by columnist Mike Royko:

   Brendan Hodges was a young musician, walking along Chicago streets, minding his own business until a thug made it his business to take Brendan's bass guitar. When Brendan tried to hold on to it, the thief shot the young man in the eye. Although the boy was attended by some of the city's best doctors at Cook County Hospital, his parents, Michael and Miriam Hodges, were told when they arrived that the boy might not make it.

   Immediately after meeting with the physicians, they rushed to an elevator, anxious to be at their son's bedside. The operator, though, informed them that they both needed visitors' passes. Understandably agitated, Mr. Hodges told the operator that their son was dying, hoping the urgency of the situation would settle the matter. Instead, the elevator operator accused Brendan's parents of having an "attitude." He then called for security.

Wanting to avoid further delay and a confrontation with security, Mr. Hodges attempted to get the elevator moving up to his son's floor but found the doors wouldn't close, even though he had pressed the floor button. At this point, security officers arrived, pushed Mrs. Hodges to the side and actually handcuffed her husband. They then led him off to their office, where he was forced to wait until the security lieutenant arrived. The lieutenant chastised the grieving father: "We have rules and regulations," *he informed him,* "and if we let you get away with it, we'd have to let everyone get away with it."

The officer, who had apparently received an erroneous update from someone else, charged, "You've been clowning around here since 11:00 this morning." *Mr. Hodges responded by pointing out that coming to the hospital to be with a dying child could hardly be termed* "clowning around." *He was finally released, but precious time had been lost. Brendan Hodges died the next morning.*

2. Ask small groups to discuss the questions shown on Slide 13.1, *"Discussion Questions,"* for 15 or 20 minutes.

3. Have a spokesperson from each group deliver a brief summary.

4. Close with reference to a nationally publicized incident of subordinates questioning leaders. Cite as examples Coleen Rowley, FBI agent in the Minnesota field office, and Sherron Watkins, vice president of Enron Corporation. Each of them went out on a professional limb and voiced their concerns about practices in which their superiors were engaged. Leaders are simply not always right, as shown in the example of Jim Jones, who "led" hundreds of people to their collective suicidal deaths.

VARIATION

Related Programs: In leadership programs especially, the idea of challenging the leader instead of following him or her without question is worthy of exploration. Not only should leaders expect empowered subordinates to challenge, question, and even "blow the whistle," they should welcome inquiries designed to ensure progress is being made, and made in the right direction.

DISCUSSION

- How can we develop the sensitivity required for situations involving raw human emotion?

- What immediate and far-reaching benefits might ensue from such development?

- How can an organization encourage rule-enforcement and simultaneously encourage the occasional flouting of rules?

QUOTATION

"So many gods, so many creeds, So many paths that wind and wind, While just the art of being kind is all the sad world needs."

– Ella Wheeler Wilcox, poet (1850–1919)

POINTS OF INTEREST

In their research on workplace incivility, authors Christine Pearson, Lynne Andersson, and Christine Porath cite a recent national poll in which 90 percent of respondents regarded incivility as a serious problem, one that leads to violence and the erosion of moral values.

Slide 13.1

Discussion Questions

1. What rules (policies, regulations, laws) should never be broken?

2. Which should/could be bent?

3. On what occasions?

4. Can you teach good judgment to others? If so, how?

5. How often are your organization's rules revisited/revised?

13.1

14. Ethical Corporate Citizenship
Librarians Don't Rule the World!

Approximately 15 minutes

OVERVIEW
Ethics "training" begins with ethics awareness. This exercise brings forth such awareness via pictorial images, which are then related to the corporate culture.

PURPOSE
To develop ethics awareness via imaginative depictions.

GROUP SIZE
Any size group. Participants will first work alone and then in triads.

ROOM ARRANGEMENT
No special arrangements needed.

MATERIALS
One magic marker, crayon, or colored pencil for each participant

METHOD
1. Begin with a dramatic flourish. Announce: *"Some of you may think that knowledge is power. [Pause.] You're wrong. Knowledge is **not** power. If it were, librarians would rule the world. And, we all know they don't! Einstein himself said that 'imagination is more important than knowledge.' And the venerable Tom Peters has declared, 'Imagination is the only source of real value in the new economy.'*

   "This activity will test your imaginative powers. It asks you to take 5 minutes and come up with a pictorial image of your organization's ethical climate. Do not use any words at all—just images to represent the morality level where you work. Think about your culture and what principles define it. Then, translate that definition or description into a visual image. You have 5 minutes. Please get started now."

2. Next, ask participants to form triads and to share their images and the meanings behind them.

3. Finally, lead a discussion that might provide new, improved, enhanced perceptions (and realities) of the ethical climate within participants' organizations.

VARIATION
Collect the unsigned depictions. Mount them on a wall and invite someone outside the training room (ideally, a member of senior management) to select the one he or she feels most accurately depicts the existing corporate climate as far as ethics are concerned.

DISCUSSION
- If yours were an ideal ethical climate, what visual image would you use to represent it?

- What steps can/should be taken to move from the real to the ideal?

- Is there a discrepancy between the Values or Ethics Statement issued by senior management and the perceptions held by the rank and file?

- If so, how can the gap be closed?

QUOTATION
"Clay is molded to make a vessel, but the utility of the vessel lies in the space where there is nothing. Thus, taking advantage of what is, we recognize the utility of what is not."

– Lao Tzu, philosopher (circa 600 B.C.E.)

POINTS OF INTEREST
When the metaphorical vessel of trust has been cracked, it's nearly impossible to make whole again. Extending the image to the Enron board of directors, we find reporters Matt Krantz and Noelle Knox noting that board members serve to ensure the company is run well. They act on shareholders' behalf. When members of the board (or members of any other group) fail to live up to their duty, they soon become *personae non gratae*. Reputations go before, during, and after the fall of trust.

15. Ethical Corporate Citizenship
It's for a Good Cause

Approximately 20 minutes

OVERVIEW
This exercise presents five all-too-familiar workplace scenarios and challenges participants to explore the ramifications of all-too-familiar reactions to those scenarios.

PURPOSE
To encourage more ethical behavior with little things, which, when considered as a totality, are immensely costly for the organization.

GROUP SIZE
Any number of participants can work on this exercise, which initially involves individual work and then small group discussions.

ROOM ARRANGEMENT
No special arrangements are required other than seating that permits seats to be rearranged to form small groups.

MATERIALS
Handout 15.1, *"Everybody Does It"*

PROCEDURE
1. Lead a discussion of "cognitive dissonance," a psychological term that refers to ways we justify information that runs contrary to our values. For example, we all know it's wrong to steal, but many of us would be willing to take company tape or clips or paper for our own use. To resolve the dissonance that results from doing something we know is wrong, we might say to ourselves, *"It only costs a penny,"* or *"They'll never miss it,"* or *"This is a small compensation for the pay raise I didn't get."* (Worse yet, some would not even feel the dissonance: they simply take the item without even thinking about it.)

2. Ask for other examples from the national scene: How did Democrats, for example, resolve the dissonance that evolved from having the president involved in an intern scandal. How do Catholics resolve the dissonance that evolves from priest pedophile charges?

3. Explain that you'd like to explore the issue further via workplace examples.

4. Distribute Handout 15.1, *"Everybody Does It,"* and allow about 15 minutes for completion.

5. Form small groups and have participants share their responses.

6. Bring closure to the exercise by asking for a spokesperson from each group to present a synopsis of the discussion.

VARIATION
Ask for a volunteer to calculate the potential cost of each scenario by:

1. Passing out small sheets of paper after the first scenario and asking each participant to anonymously indicate whether or not he or she has used the company's fax machine or copy machine for his or her own purposes.

2. Obtaining a percentage reflecting the number of people, compared to the class total, who do employ company property for their own use. On the same sheet, ask each person to indicate the number of times in a given year that he or she uses the company fax machine or copy machine for personal use.

3. Calculating the cost of such action in terms of lost productivity.

4. Multiplying that cost times the number of times it is likely to happen in a given year for a single employee.

5. Multiplying that cost times the number of employees in the organization.

6. Multiplying that cost by the percentage of employees who are likely to engage in such conduct.

DISCUSSION
- What characteristics will business leaders need for success a decade from now?

- What are some of the reasons people give for small violations of ethics?

- Is it worth a manager's time to attempt to put an end to such violations?

- Assume you are the head of the department or head of the company. What would you say to end such "conversion-thefts"?

QUOTATION
"Anything you do is everything you do."

– Buddhist saying

POINTS OF INTEREST

"Profitability and the Common Good," an article by Pam Mayer, reports an interesting study from the Johnson School of Management at Cornell University. The School surveyed executives from several Fortune 1000 companies and asked, *"What characteristics will business leaders need for success a decade from now?"* The top two answers from these executives were **teambuilding** and **compassion.**

The same question was asked of MBA students from the top 20 business schools. Their responses related to profitability: the trait they selected was an orientation toward results. (Only 28 percent of the students strongly agreed that corporations have a responsibility to the environment. Half the executives were in strong agreement with the statement.)

Handout 15.1
"Everybody Does It"

Directions

We all realize that a clerk taking money from the cash register is stealing; that the Enron and Global Crossing scandals, in which insider information was used for personal profit and to mislead the public, are morally wrong. But in the commonplace occurrences of our everyday lives, do we stop to think about the small ways in which our integrity is put to the test? Read each of these scenarios and answer the questions related to them as honestly as possible.

1. Your child's school calls you at work, because you forgot to turn in a signed permission slip for today's field trip. The school secretary offers to fax you one to sign; your return of the signed paper will permit your child to join his classmates. If not, a sad face will greet you after a day of being left behind at school, while everyone else had a great time.

    What do you do?

    _____

    What is your employer's policy on personal fax use?

    _____

    Would it be different if the fax involved a long-distance call? Why or why not?

    _____

    _____

    Would the situation be different if the fax were for a car loan application, student loan paperwork, or an RSVP to a retirement dinner? If so, tell how, in reference to each of these three situations.

    _____

    _____

    _____

    _____

    _____

    _____

Handout 15.1: *Everybody Does It* (continued)

2.   You're responsible for making flyers for the PTA bake sale. Would you copy
     them on the company copier? If so, what would your rationale be?

     _____

     _____

     _____

     What is your employer's policy on personal use of the copier?

     _____

     Would it matter if you brought your own paper?

     _____

     Would it matter if it were for a charity, as opposed to something for private
     gain, like **"For Sale"** flyers for your used computer?

     _____

3.   Most employers have policies covering local phone calls. If yours does, do
     they limit the times when calls can be made or accepted? If local calls are
     acceptable, is there an issue with the amount of time spent on the phone, as
     opposed to phone charges? Share your views here of what is or, perhaps, what
     should be allowed.

     _____

     _____

     _____

     _____

4.   Think of a scenario involving actions that might be described as being in a
     "gray zone." The scenario could be related to checking personal e-mail while
     at work, using the Internet to shop or bank online, favoring a friend in a hiring
     or promotion situation, or something similar. Tell the consequences of these
     actions, specifying, if you can, how "innocent" things can lead to trouble
     (gossip, damaged reputations, reprimands, etc.).

     _____

     _____

     _____

     _____

Handout 15.1: *Everybody Does It* (concluded)

5. What overall conclusions can be drawn about habits and the "everybody does it" syndrome at work?

    _____

    _____

    _____

    _____

The fancy legal term for much of the above is "theft by conversion," or using someone else's property without asking for permission in order to meet your own needs. Even if you don't agree that all of the examples given above are wrong, ask yourself how you would react if you read in the newspaper that employees of your children's school or the City Hall were engaged in such actions and getting paid by your tax dollars. Remember, it's what we do when no one is looking that truly shows our character (and in the digital age, somebody is probably looking).

Submitted by: Lloyd A. Conway, Academic Coordinator
                Spring Arbor University
                4920 Wainwright
                Lansing MI 49811
                517-393-8415
                ssgConway@juno.com

16. Ethical Corporate Citizenship
Flirting with Danger

Approximately 75 minutes

OVERVIEW
Participants are encouraged to think about the ethical ramifications of seemingly innocent acts, such as flirtatious behaviors, sexual innuendoes, seductive remarks and/or invitations.

PURPOSE
To make participants aware of personal and organizational liabilities that follow certain actions.

GROUP SIZE
Ideal group size would be 18 to 20 participants, subdivided into groups of 4 or 5.

ROOM ARRANGEMENT
If possible, table groups divided into separate workstations.

MATERIALS
- Equipment for displaying PowerPoint slides
- Slide 16.1, *"Gender Dynamics in the Workplace"*
- Slide 16.2, *"Definition: Gender Dynamics"*
- Slide 16.3, *"Definition: Boundary"*
- Bright-colored Post-it® notes
- Masking tape
- Flipchart with the following headings written at the top of the first three pages (see next page):

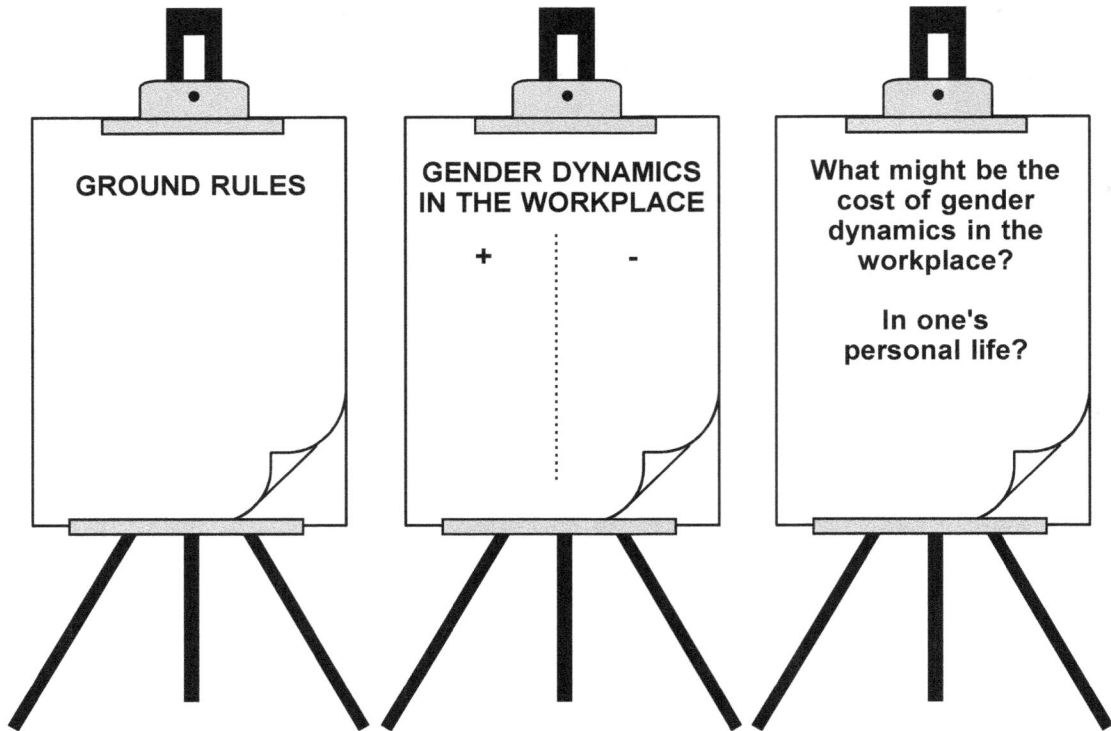

GROUND RULES

GENDER DYNAMICS IN THE WORKPLACE

+ | -

What might be the cost of gender dynamics in the workplace?

In one's personal life?

PROCEDURE

1. Display Slide 16.1, *"Gender Dynamics in the Workplace,"* as participants arrive in the classroom. Introduce yourself and ask participants to do the same. Introduce the topic of gender dynamics and ask for (and/or provide) a few short examples such as "flirtatious behaviors," "sexual innuendoes," "seductive remarks," "unsolicited hugs."

2. Turn to the **Ground Rules** page on the flipchart. List your expectations of participants and ask them to share their expectations of you.

3. Ask the group to define "gender dynamics." Following a brief discussion, offer the definition that appears on Slide 16.2, *"Gender Dynamics."*

4. Ask small groups to discuss the topic by exploring both the positive and negative implications of this form of energy in a workplace setting. One spokesperson per group will then verbalize the group discussion and write the key points on the second flipchart page.

5. On separate Post-it® notes, participants will each list five behaviors they engage in, or perhaps have been invited to engage in, at work. Ask for volunteers to share their lists and then ask that they be posted on the wall or on a new flipchart page.

6. Lead a large-group discussion using the Post-it® notes on the wall or flipchart. Begin a new page, based on this discussion, of implications or possible consequences that might result from this behavior.

7. Turn to the third flipchart page and continue the discussion by noting answers to the question written at the top: **What might be the cost of gender dynamics in the workplace?**

8. Conclude by facilitating a large-group discussion regarding the importance of having healthy boundaries in workplace environments. Ask what a boundary is. Display Slide 16.3, *"Definition: Boundary,"* and share this definition of a "boundary" in gender-dynamics terms: *"It's an understanding of where you and another person begin and end; it's the specification of a limit, personally and professionally."*

9. Raise these questions as well: *"Would you entertain these behaviors"* (identified in #5) *in the presence of your or the other person's significant other?" "Would you entertain them in the presence of other work colleagues?"*

10. Point out that what you *truthfully* recognize as a gray area or an area of "danger" is an area in which you are likely to transgress boundaries. Encourage participants to follow this process of thinking about costs and questions and boundaries the next time, and every time, they encounter gray areas.

VARIATION

Work to devise other questions for other aspects of the work environment. For example, when considering what customers expect/want/deserve, ask, "If the customer could see what I'm doing right now, would the customer be willing to pay for it?" When wondering if a given action is something that falls within the boundaries of ethical leadership, the question might be, "If this action were to appear as a headline in tomorrow's newspaper, would I still proceed with it?"

DISCUSSION

• What's the most efficient way to enhance creative energy while maintaining healthy collegial boundaries?

• Should these boundaries be monitored? If so, how? Should policies be created regarding such boundaries?

• Do employers have the right to address sexually energized behaviors in the workplace?

• Where does the workplace environment begin and end?

QUOTATION
"To love is to admire with the heart; to admire is to love with the mind."
– Theophile Gautier

POINTS OF INTEREST
As illustrated in *Successful Meetings*, an inappropriate illustration of gender dynamics cost a top Fox Television executive his job. In a prepared speech delivered to a conference of 200 executives in Snowmass, Colorado, in June, 1992, Stephen Chao wanted to make the point that violence was more obscene than nudity and sexuality. As planned, a young man whom Chao had hired appeared beside the speaker, completely naked. Immediately after his presentation, Chao was confronted by Rupert Murdoch, who fired him on the spot. As Murdoch later explained, *"There's one thing this company must make clear—that there are limits."*

Submitted by: Eve Strella and Gwen Martone
                 Illuminate of Rochester, Inc.
                 15 Stuyvesant Road
                 Suite 100
                 Pittsford, New York 14534
                 Phone and fax: 585-385-9699
                 E-mail: estrella@thexlr8team.com
                 Web site: www.lightyourpath.com

Illuminate of Rochester, Inc., is a coaching, consulting, training, and team development organization whose focus is to assist individuals and organizations in transition through issues of change, layoffs, mergers, abusive management and co-worker behavior, and fear in the workplace. Co-CEOs Eve Strella and Gwen Martone have merged their expertise as an industrial engineer and a clinical therapist with a combined 32 years of hands-on experience in the area of human solutions.

Slide 16.1

Gender Dynamics in the Workplace

16.1

Slide 16.2

Gender Dynamics

Refers to the energy exchanged between members of the same or opposite sex. These exchanges are often charged with some degree of tension, however slight, and are usually characterized as flirtatious in nature.

16.2

Slide 16.3

Boundary

An understanding of where you and another person begin and end; the specification of a limit, personally and professionally.

16.3

17. Ethical Corporate Citizenship
Leader of the PAC

Approximately 45 minutes

OVERVIEW
Participants in this exercise, based on an actual corporate practice, answer a series of questions related to a new-hire situation. Then they discuss the pros and cons of a particular course of action.

PURPOSE
To provide alternatives to actions that may be troublesome.

GROUP SIZE
Any size group can work on this exercise.

ROOM ARRANGEMENT
No special arrangement required.

MATERIALS
Handout 17.1, *"Leader of the PAC"*

PROCEDURE
1. Ask the group what they know/how they feel about campaign contributions and the ethical issues they raise.

2. Distribute Handout 17.1, *"Leader of the PAC,"* and ask participants to answer the questions on the bottom.

3. After about 15 minutes, have participants form small groups to prepare a script that has a newly hired employee actually explain to his or her manager that he or she prefers not to participate in the program.

4. Have each group present to one other group and obtain feedback on the effectiveness of the scripted presentation. Then the second group will make its presentation to the group that has just presented and will receive feedback from them. (**Note:** If there is an odd number of groups, have the "odd" group present to the entire class and then meet with you in a breakout room or a corner of the classroom. If the other groups are still working after you've provided feedback, split your group up: each person will join a different group and sit in as an observer.)

5. Lead a discussion about the need to speak up for what one believes is right juxtaposed with the need to be realistic in an "office-politics" setting.

6. Conclude by challenging participants to come up with an original three- or four-word original phrase that simply inspires. (Examples could be "Never give up," "Just do it," and "Just say no.") Post their declarations around the room.

VARIATION
To illustrate the delicate balance required as managers walk the corporate tightrope, ask half the groups to write the script from the viewpoint of a manager who's been told by his or her own manager that his or her performance appraisal depends, in part, on the amount of money contributed by his or her department to Political Action Committees. They should assume the manager sees nothing wrong with campaign contributions, as he or she honestly believes they help protect jobs.

DISCUSSION
- Why do you think there's been so much resistance to campaign reform?

- Will efforts to influence political leaders disappear now that reform is official? Explain your answer. Draw a line in the middle of a sheet of paper. List on the left all the reasons why a new hire might hesitate to express his or her opposition to such contributions. On the right, list all the reasons why he or she might "go along to get along."

QUOTATION
"There may be times when we are powerless to prevent injustice, but there must never be a time when we fail to protest."
                                                    – Elie Wiesel

POINTS OF INTEREST
The McCain-Feingold Campaign Finance Reform Bill, passed by Congress in March 2002, was propelled by people such as Russell Feingold, who feel that the overhaul of campaign finance was sorely needed. Feingold has publicly referred to soft money as a "taint" on the democracy. "Soft money" refers to the no-holds-barred contributions wealthy individuals, corporations, and labor unions can make to political parties. In theory, such money cannot be used for campaigning in federal elections. In reality, prior to the passage of new legislation targeting soft money, it was used primarily for federal elections.

Handout 17.1
Leader of the PAC

You are the successful candidate (the final "short list" had twelve contenders) for a job that you've dreamed of all your life. It's your first day now with a company that leases buildings to the federal government. As you're settling in, your supervisor approaches, shakes your hand, and then gives you the following letter:

> The Rogert Employee Political Action Committee (REPAC) welcomes you to our organization. As you may know, only administrative, executive, managerial, and professional personnel, like yourself, who are earning more than $70,000 annually are invited to participate in REPAC.
>
> Of course, Rogert, Inc., does not show favoritism toward those who do not join REPAC. Nor do we consider the amount contributed when promotional decisions are made and/or career opportunities are extended. The program is entirely voluntary. However, it is important to know that our dollars have helped protect property-management jobs: to date, every single one of our buildings has at least two tenants leasing a minimum of 90,000 square feet of space.
>
> Please call us if you have questions. Your assistance and cooperation are appreciated. Know that Rogert senior management remains committed to involving key people in the political process. That process is paramount to our people and their jobs.

1. What sentences, if any, do you find troublesome?

    _____

    _____

2. What questions does this letter evoke?

    _____

    _____

3. Would you be likely to call the person who wrote this letter to get answers to those questions? Why or why not?

    _____

    _____

Handout 17.1: *Leader of the PAC* (concluded)

4.   Would you join REPAC? Explain your decision. _____

_____

_____

5.   Would you make a donation? If not, why not? If so, why and how much?

_____

_____

_____

Additional comments: _____

_____

_____

Reproduced from *50 Reproducible Activities for Promoting Ethics Within the Organization*,
by Marlene Caroselli. HRD Press, 2015.

18. Ethical Corporate Citizenship
Lobbying for Positions

Approximately 15 minutes

OVERVIEW
This exercise asks participants to design an ethics-based question that might help job applicants self-screen before making important decisions.

PURPOSE
- To develop the "irreducible essence" of a company.
- To help participants clarify values.

GROUP SIZE
Any size group, which will be divided into subgroups of three or four.

ROOM ARRANGEMENT
No special arrangement required.

MATERIALS
- Flipchart
- Marking pens

PROCEDURE
1. Introduce the exercise by writing on the flipchart: "Do you believe America should be building weapons of mass destruction? If not, you shouldn't be applying for a job with this company." Explain that, according to one urban legend, a large West Coast defense contractor has this sign prominently displayed in its lobby, right outside the entrance to the Human Resources department, where applicants would have to go to be interviewed. From the get-go, the company wants prospective employees to be fully aware of what the company does. They realize that if applicants feel the company product is immoral, they simply should not be considering employment there.

2. Ask participants to consider what Senator Hubert Humphrey referred to as an "irreducible essence," i.e., when all else is stripped away, what is your fundamental core, your basic essence, the unshakeable element that remains? For Humphrey, it was love of country. For individuals and organizations alike, the essence-question is an important one to ask. Elicit a few responses for participants or perhaps provide your own.

3. Now have participants think about what it is their organization stands for or does. (If the group has several people who work in the same organization, they may wish to work together on this question.)

4. Once they've determined their organization's *raison d'être*, task them with asking a question and then supplying an answer similar to the one described in step 1 above.

5. Have small groups discuss whether the essence question (and answer) conflicts with their personal values. If so, invite them to discuss what, if anything, they intend to do about this potential conflict in values.

VARIATION

Invite participants to consider what it is they stand for—as a man, as a woman, as an employee, as a manager, as a team member, as an American, et cetera. Have them draft a letter sharing what they've learned over the years about values in a workplace setting. The recipient of the letter is a hypothetical new employee.

Urge the person responsible for new-employee orientation to include some of these letters in the orientation brochure.

DISCUSSION

- How much congruence exists between what you value and what your organization/department/department head values? If a gap exists, how troubled are you by it?

- How widely disseminated are your organization's values?

- Other than the need to earn a paycheck, what keeps people in places that don't reflect their personally held values?

QUOTATION

"The palest ink is better than the best memory."

– Chinese proverb

POINTS OF INTEREST

When there's a lack of congruence between a company's public statement and its private practice, everyone suffers. Such was the case with Wal-Mart's "Made Right Here" proclamation, as reported by Keri Hayes. Along with 17 other companies, Wal-Mart was named in a class-action lawsuit, filed on behalf of 50,000 employees in Saipan (where, according to a Department of Interior spokesman, pregnant women were coerced to have abortions or to lose their jobs). The National Labor Committee found that 85 percent of Wal-Mart's private-label merchandise was not "made right here," but rather, was manufactured in other countries.

19. Ethical Corporate Citizenship
Neutron Neutrality

Approximately 25 minutes

OVERVIEW
Based on an article regarding a job-loss suicide, this exercise asks participants to consider ways to make job-loss less negative and more neutral, if not positive.

PURPOSE
To engender creative ideas for making job-loss less traumatic.

GROUP SIZE
Any size group. Participants will first work alone and then in subgroups of four or five.

ROOM ARRANGEMENT
No special arrangement required other than seating flexible enough to permit small-group formations.

MATERIALS
Handout 19.1, *"Termination Facts"*; articles about Jack Welch obtained or downloaded in advance of class

METHOD
1. Start the exercise by asking if anyone has read *Straight from the Gut*, the biography of General Electric's (GE) former CEO, Jack Welch. Engage the group in a brief discussion about Welch and some of the policies he's instituted at General Electric (such as the Work-Out). Also have them discuss some of the remarks for which he's famous ("When the rate of change outside the company is greater than the rate of change inside the company, then we are looking at the beginning of the end"). Note that while he's been called the Manager of the Century, he's also been called Neutron Jack, for policies that leave buildings standing but people decimated.

2. Explain that one of those policies—to cut costs whenever and wherever possible—is highlighted in their handout. Ask participants to read the facts related to GE's termination procedure at Erie Works and then to answer the questions on the handout.

3. Distribute Handout 19.1, *"Termination Facts,"* and ask everyone to work on it individually.

4. Then have participants work in groups of four or five to come up with at least five ways to make terminations less painful. Encourage full use of their creative talents as they consider suicide-preventive measures as well as supportive overtures the organization can extend to laid-off workers.

5. Have a reporter from each group write the group's ideas on flipchart paper, to be posted around the room.

6. Bring closure by asking, "How many of you have lost a job at least once in your life?" "How many feel that subsequent jobs were even better than the one you lost?" "How can this information be shared with employees who face termination?" Have a scribe record the ideas and add them to the ideas listed in the preceding step.

7. Ask for a volunteer to disseminate the ideas to anyone within the organization who has responsibility for advising employees they are being terminated.

VARIATION
Show the value of the Work-Out session by adapting it to classroom use as follows:

"We've got to take out the boss element," says Jack Welch, General Electric's former CEO. Managers, he asserts, have to give up their old powers of planning, organizing, implementing, and measuring, and assume some new duties: counseling groups, providing them resources, helping them think for themselves. He encourages empowerment, and asks workers to challenge authority in an echo of Tom Peters' assertion that "if you have gone a whole week without being disobedient, you are doing yourself and the organization a disservice."

Determined to get rid of management styles that suppress or intimidate, Welch decreed that managers either buy in to the empowerment afforded by Work-Outs or else they'd be fired.

Work-Out sessions have proven to be enormously profitable, on many levels beyond the interpersonal. Welch encourages employees to take the work out of work. On another level, the sessions help employees work out their problems. And, the sessions, like their aerobic counterparts, make the organization leaner and stronger.

Work-Out steps include:

1. Choose issue(s) to discuss.

2. Select a cross-functional team appropriate for the problem.

3. Choose a champion who will help recommendations become reality.

4. Let the team meet for three days (or as needed) to draw up recommendations for improving processes.

5. Meet with the manager who must respond with "yes," "no," or "maybe" to recommendations on the spot. Reasons/details are provided for each decision.

6. Hold additional meetings as needed to pursue recommendations.

7. Continue the process with these and other issues.

These steps, adapted for the classroom learning situation, ask you to divide into four groups. Then, each person in the group will quickly name (but not discuss) a solvable work-related problem. The problem group members will ultimately select should be one that—once solved or resolved—will help each person meet his or her goals. (Be prepared to tell what they are.) The problem should also be one that advances the organizational mission. (Be prepared to specify what that is.)

As you listen to your group members, don't offer solutions to the problems you hear described. Instead, allow each person to state the problem so that it is clearly understood by the others in the group. Questions are allowed, but only for the purpose of clarification, not for solution-seeking.

Then, as a group, select the one problem that most needs attention. The "owner" of the problem will present it to another group and will then leave the room while the group to which the problem was presented discusses feasible solutions. (Observers will note the extent of positive and negative interpersonal exchanges.) Your group will work to find five or more possible solutions for the problem that the problem-owner presented to you.

When the owner returns, your group will present its suggested solutions. The owner must immediately decide to accept (with a rationale), reject (with reasons), or table (with an explanation of why and when) each of the solutions. An observing team (represented by senior management in the real world) later meets with the owner.

Four of you will serve as observers—one for each of the reporting teams. Your first assignment is to observe the interactions among the teams attempting to find solutions for the owner's problem. The team should come up with at least five possibilities. Look for interpersonal/group dynamics examples of:

Positive Behaviors	Negative Behaviors
Leadership	Domination of the discussion
Creativity	Belittling remarks
Harmony	Poor listening
Full participation	Side conversations

As soon as the team has prepared a list of suggestions/solutions, share your observations with them.

Your second assignment requires you to observe the "owner's" reaction to the team's suggestions. Did he or she, for example, take notes? Was he or she defensive? Did he or she give realistic responses? What did you learn about the "owner" by watching his or her responses to the suggestions of the team?

Four "owners" will read articles about the GE Work-Outs and will have a 5 to 10 minute report ready. The report will describe Work-Outs in greater detail and the benefits they're designed to create.

DISCUSSION
- What other public figures can you recall who are highly regarded despite what many consider serious flaws?

- What lies behind people's willingness to regard such people so highly?

- What does it say about our national tolerance for unethical behavior when we read lists such as the one that appears in the Points of Interest?

QUOTATION
"A mind all logic is like a knife all blade. It makes the hand bleed that uses it."
– Rabindranath Tagore

POINTS OF INTEREST
While we cannot attest to the accuracy of the following Internet circulation, we suspect it contains a great deal of truth. If nothing else, read it for its amusement value. If you are inclined toward investigation, attempt to verify the truth of the statements.

Imagine working for a company that has a little more than 500 employees and has the following statistics:

- 29 have been accused of spousal abuse
- 7 have been arrested for fraud
- 19 have been accused of writing bad checks

- 117 have directly or indirectly bankrupted at least two businesses
- 3 have done time for assault
- 71 cannot get a credit card due to bad credit
- 14 have been arrested on drug-related charges
- 8 have been arrested for shoplifting
- 21 are currently defendants in lawsuits
- 84 have been arrested for drunk driving within the last year

Can you guess which organization this is?

Give up yet?

It's the 535 members of the United States Congress! The same group that cranks out hundreds of new laws each year designed to keep the rest of us in line.

Handout 19.1
Termination Facts

Directions

Read these facts, excerpted from an article by Thomas O'Boyle. Then answer the questions that follow:

- At Erie Works, a General Electric (GE) site, Ivan Winebrenner, age 39, received a termination notice on June 10, 1993. He was one of 200 workers who were let go because of "lack of work."

- Two days later, his wife found him dead in their bedroom from a gunshot wound to the head.

- Two days after this discovery, co-worker Anthony Victor Torelli turned a gun on himself, having failed to find his foreman at the plant. There have been several suicides since among the ranks of the Erie Works plant.

- Engineering supervisor at the plant, Sheldon Potter, who quit rather than participate in the layoffs, describes the process as "totally inhuman in any other context."

- Employees at this GE site were given laminated cards with a statement of GE's Beliefs—the first of which is "People, working together, are the source of our strength."

- In the year when the suicides occurred, Erie Works had recorded its best profits ever.

- The layoffs were the result of a corporate decision to convert the manufacture of locomotive parts from an in-house production to the purchase of these parts from an outside vendor.

- GE's former CEO moved the company from eleventh in stock value among American corporations to first place.

- In the streamlining process, 300,000 people lost their jobs.

How humane do you feel your company's termination policy is?

If you were a CEO, driven to produce profits for shareholders and other stake-holders, what would your top priority be?

119

Handout 19.1: *Termination Facts* (concluded)

Is it unethical for an organization to engage in cost-cutting—even if it means job-loss?

How can the termination process be made more humane?

20. Ethical Corporate Citizenship
Whatever It Takes

Approximately 25 minutes

OVERVIEW
For participants who have been caught between company loyalty and a private morality, this exercise, based on an actual event, illustrates the difficulty and possible consequences of "doing the right thing." For those who have not yet had that experience, the exercise affords an opportunity for advance preparation.

PURPOSE
- To explore the ramifications of defying a manager's suggestion.
- To provide ideas for achieving clarity regarding job expectations.

GROUP SIZE
Any size group, divided into subgroups of four or five.

ROOM ARRANGEMENT
No special arrangement required other than seating flexible enough to permit small groups to be formed.

MATERIALS
- Flipchart
- Marking pens
- Handout 20.1, *"Checklist"*
- Handout 20.2, *"Whatever It Takes"*

PROCEDURE
1. Ask participants to complete Handout 20.1 and to share some of their answers with a partner.

2. Lead into the next part of the exercise by alluding to some of the questions on the checklist and noting that a lack of communication can lead us into difficult or uncomfortable positions. Usually, because of our background and experience, we're able to handle those challenges with no adverse repercussions. In truth, we sometimes emerge from those conflicts stronger than we were before encountering them. Other times, though, the situations are so dangerous that potential harm could befall any number of parties involved. Ask participants to reflect on some situations they've experienced that could be described this way. In groups of four or five, have them share those experiences.

121

3. Distribute Handout 20.2 and have the same groups read and discuss the case study.

4. Wrap the exercise up by asking for input from each group. This input will correlate one sentence from the checklist with answers to one of the questions on the case-study handout.

VARIATION

*   Elicit other difficult scenarios. Record them on the flipchart and assign one to each small group. They'll develop role-plays based on them. After each is enacted, elicit feedback from the whole group regarding lines that were especially effective.

*   Encourage participants to answer these questions:

    What obstacles prevent me from doing the best job of which I am capable?

    If I were to leave tomorrow, what knowledge/skills/abilities would the person who replaces me need to have?

    What is the best thing about this organization?

    No organization is perfect. In what way does this organization most need to improve?

    Then, have participants give the same questions to their managers to answer. They should schedule a time when the two sets of answers can be compared.

DISCUSSION

*   Have you given conscious thought to the boundaries you won't cross—no matter what the consequences?

*   What are some of the unspoken expectations associated with your job—both your expectations and your manager's?

*   In what circumstances were your principles compromised?

*   What other examples do you know of when someone's principles were compromised? What was the result of this compromise?

QUOTATION
"We are all born originals. Why is it so many of us die copies?"
– Edward Young

POINTS OF INTEREST
In the case of *Pullum v. Hudson Foods Inc.,* 871 S.W. 2d 94 (Missouri), Pullum was engaged in horseplay when she should have been working. Company policy clearly forbids such actions. When a co-worker threw something at her, Pullum retaliated and was injured in the process. She sued for compensation benefits, which the company sought to deny, stating that she was engaged in an activity that was expressly forbidden.

The courts awarded Pullum compensation benefits, asserting that her foolish and negligent behavior was irrelevant in light of the injuries sustained.

Handout 20.1
Checklist

YES   NO

☐   ☐   I meet regularly with my manager to discuss my career path.

☐   ☐   I am fully aware of organizational policies.

☐   ☐   My manager and I have discussed the worst mistake I could possibly make as far as this job is concerned.

☐   ☐   I know what my manager values.

☐   ☐   I'm cognizant of the inherent dangers of my job.

☐   ☐   I regularly consider worst-case scenarios related to my job and have appropriate courses of action ready.

☐   ☐   I could prioritize the organization's top five values.

☐   ☐   The training I receive is based on an assessment of my strengths and weaknesses.

☐   ☐   The things I have learned about this organization since being hired lead me to respect it more than I originally did.

☐   ☐   I could easily nominate my organization as one of the best 100 American organizations.

☐   ☐   Expectations are clearly stated here.

☐   ☐   My manager shares information with his or her staff regularly.

Reproduced from *50 Reproducible Activities for Promoting Ethics Within the Organization*, by Marlene Caroselli. HRD Press, 2015.

Handout 20.2
Whatever It Takes

The Situation
Pam is a confident, self-assured young woman, a former model who "retired" from that career at age 30 to enter the world of sales. She's been moderately successful selling business systems to corporations and is now having a business dinner in the dining room of a four-star hotel. The meeting is going well until the prospective buyer suggests they go up to his room for an after-dinner drink. She demurs, but the client becomes insistent—going so far as to suggest the six-digit sale is dependent on an affirmative answer.

"You think about it while I go to the men's room," he tells her and then excuses himself from the table. Pam immediately calls her boss on his cell phone and reports the dilemma. His advice: "Do whatever it takes to get that sale."

1. Had you been Pam, what would you have done?

    _____

    _____

    _____

    _____

    _____

    _____

    _____

2. What are some possible consequences of the different choices Pam could have made?

    _____

    _____

    _____

    _____

    _____

    _____

    _____

Handout 20.2: *Whatever It Takes* (concluded)

3. How much clarity is there, on your part and your manager's, regarding job expectations? When was the last time the two of you met to discuss those (changing) expectations?

    _____

    _____

    _____

    _____

    _____

    _____

4. What do you know now about your job that you wish you had known then (when you were first hired)?

    _____

    _____

    _____

    _____

    _____

    _____

Part C:
Ethical Salesmanship
Introduction: Robin Wilson

"Greatness is not found in possessions, power, position or prestige. It is discovered in goodness, humility, service, and character."

– William Mead

The search for acquiring possessions and the desire for a new position or greater power often puts blinders on a person's eyes. We live in a society in which the attitude is "more is better," causing some people to temporarily set aside their ethics and values. Salespeople will overpromise and yet underdeliver in their quest for a big job or a new client. People may reason with themselves and say that doing an inadequate job once or twice is really "not a big deal" or "it doesn't hurt anyone in the long run." They may also stretch the truth or badmouth a competitor in hopes of getting a sale.

The world is a different place now. Customers may expect more than they did a few years ago. People are smarter and savvier; they expect to be treated honestly and fairly. Companies that lose sight of their essential core values will not be around for the long haul.

In the current job market, many companies are restructuring and laying off at an accelerated rate. More and more pressure is being put on various sales departments to bring in more revenue. This can create underlying fear and frustration that often results in a lack of caring, resulting in lower standards and compromising of values.

A recent survey stated that in a group of 18- to 34-year-olds, 79 percent believed that there were no absolute ethical standards. To some, this statistic may seem high, yet it may easily reflect the changes plaguing companies in the last few years. In response to increased competition, decreased market share, and lower sales, ethics have become compromised.

For example, in one company, everyone was hearing about the company's focus on principles and values. This topic was talked about at every level and practiced by management. The CEO thought his job was to instill his core principles and beliefs to all levels of management. He thought that if each employee felt and lived by those values, customers would feel comfortable. They would trust the company and ultimately sales would increase. This company grew to $1 billion in annual revenue in a relatively short time. Since then, a management company took over and those core values were abandoned. The result was decreased sales and increased competition. This story is not unique to one company, but often heard and played out throughout many organizations.

In this time of increasing change and competition, what is the answer? The long-term solution is rooted in clearly stated values and ethics that are practiced on a daily basis. The company needs to define and communicate its vision, values, and principles. These values must be explained and clearly understood by the sales team. They need to be part of the sales presentation so that customers can understand them. Mutual trust is essential in building a foundation within a company and it must become an equally shared principle. If a company communicates and practices its core values, employees will feel greater security, caring, and belief in the product. Ultimately, this feeling will reflect their attitude and customers will know it.

As a society, we view success by a person's material wealth and that makes sales and ethics almost an oxymoron. Long-term success in sales can only be gained and consequently retained by building trusting relationships. By adhering to strong values and ethics, salespeople can keep their minds open, building confidence and creativity to create new and better opportunities.

Submitted by: Robin Wilson
                  Reach and Achieve Associates
                  26 Butternut Drive
                  Pittsford, New York 14534
                  Phone: 585-218-9350
                  Fax: 585-248-2117
                  E-mail: Robin@ReachandAchieve.com
                  Web site: www.ReachandAchieve.com

Reach and Achieve Associates provides professional coaching and training to individuals, staff, and management of businesses of all sizes. Partner with us to create and implement strategies for developing stronger people and organizations.

21. Ethical Salesmanship
A Stick in Time Saves Nine

Approximately 20 minutes (more or less, depending on size of class)

OVERVIEW
Using any one of nine common phrases about sticks, participants will select one and relate it to the ethical position taken by their corporate leaders.

PURPOSE
To develop insight concerning the ethical climate by regarding it from a fresh perspective.

GROUP SIZE
Any size group.

ROOM ARRANGEMENT
If possible, table groups for four participants.

MATERIALS
- Equipment for displaying PowerPoint slides
- Slide 21.1, *"Nine 'Stick' Phrases"*

METHOD
1. Introduce this activity with the proviso that what is said in the room remains in the room. Advise the group that you'd like them to protect the innocent—and perhaps the guilty—by working on an exercise that asks them to project the ethical positions of organizational leaders. However, you'd like them not to identify any one person by name.

2. Explain that one of the best ways to garner original insights is to juxtapose two unrelated things. To that end, you'd like them to think in terms of "sticks" and to relate a "stick" phrase to the company's sales philosophy, predicated on the declaration of its leaders.

3. Divide the group into subgroups of four or five participants and show Slide 21.1, *"Nine 'Stick' Phrases."* Explain that you'd like them to select any one of the phrases and relate it to the organization's sales philosophy. If they respond that there *is* no such philosophy, ask them to create one and then to continue with the exercise.

4. Appoint a spokesperson from each group to meet in a breakout room or a corner of the room and to synthesize their reports in a creative fashion. They might compose a poem, a rhyme, a rap song. They might illustrate their discussion using symbols on the flipchart. They might even make a sales "pitch" to the rest of the group, encouraging them to buy in to the corporate sales philosophy.

5. As that group is working, write the word E-T-H-I-C-S along the top of the flipchart and make columns (six, in all) beneath each letter. Divide the remaining participants into six groups and challenge them to come up with as many words, related to ethical sales, as they can think of. Each word must begin with the letter ("E," "T," "H," "I," "C," or "S") assigned to them.

6. While you wait for the synthesizing spokespersons to complete their assignment, call on each team (in continued rotation, if need be) to select one word and explain to the rest of the class its ethical significance.

7. Bring closure to the exercise by having the synthesizing team make their presentation.

VARIATION
- Ask the group to come up with additional "stick" phrases, such as:

Can't beat it with a stick	*Stick with it*
End up with the short end of the stick	*Stick out like a sore thumb*
Get on the stick	*Stick to your knitting*
Get the short end of the stick	*Stick together*
Quicker than you can shake a stick at it	*Stick up for him*
Stick 'em up	*Stick your foot in your mouth*
Stick around	*Stick your neck out*
Stick by him	*Stick your nose in where it doesn't*
Stick in your craw	*belong*
Stick it out	

Then ask small groups to select one of the posted phrases and relate it to the ethical climate of a larger institution: e.g., the presidency, Wall Street financiers, corporate America, the Olympics, the Catholic Church, the automotive industry, etc.

- Invite participants to form committees to either create or revise the organizational sales philosophy.

DISCUSSION

- To what extent do the values of the organizational head cascade down to the average employee?

- How difficult would it be for you to challenge the tone (positive or negative) that's been established by the head of your organization?

- What's the connection in your organization between sales and ethics?

QUOTATION

"An invasion of armies can be resisted, but not an idea whose time has come."

– Victor Hugo

POINTS OF INTEREST

In *The Best Seller*, author D. Forbes Ley asserts, *"The problem here, as well as all across the profession of selling, is that few Salespeople take the time to develop any new openings. They want to stay with what they have rather than be creative and take the chance of coming up with something new and exciting."*

He suggests using the concept of mystery as a means of stimulating creative thought.

Again, it's the juxtaposition of diverse ideas that often leads to creative thinking about sales and the ethical bases on which they are made.

Slide 21.1

Nine "Stick" Phrases

1. Walk softly and carry a big stick
2. Sticks and stones won't break my bones
3. Stick in the mud
4. A carrot on a stick
5. Sticky fingers
6. Stick to your guns
7. Stick it to them
8. Stickler for details
9. Sticky wicket

21.1

22. Ethical Salesmanship
A Sale of Need Is a Sale Indeed

Approximately 25 minutes (more or less, depending on size of class)

OVERVIEW
The sales process should never be one-directional, based only on the salesperson's need to sell a product or service. This exercise illustrates the importance of involving the buyer in the selling process and of ethically considering the role of need in sales and non-sales.

PURPOSE
To encourage buyer-input while a sale is being conducted.

GROUP SIZE
Any size group, divided into subgroups of four or five.

ROOM ARRANGEMENT
If possible, table groups for four or five participants.

MATERIALS
Optional: A bag of candy

PROCEDURE
1. Hold up some common item—perhaps one that is in the room already, such as a role of masking tape or a token prize that you've purchased in advance— perhaps a dictionary or a set of marking pens.

2. Explain that you'll allow only 10 minutes for table groups to come up with a convincing sales pitch, the objective of which is to persuade you to purchase the common item you're holding. Note that one person will serve as sales spokesperson for the group.

3. After 10 minutes, call on every spokesperson in turn and allow each up to 3 minutes to make the sales pitch. Listen carefully to learn if any one of them evinces an interest in finding out what you need.

4. After all groups have made their presentation, award the prize (or ask the class to give a standing ovation) to the table group that inquired about your needs. (If more than one group did, share the candy or have several ovations. If none did, proceed with your concluding remarks.)

5. Discuss the two-way nature of successful sales: not only should salespeople focus on what they need to sell, they should also focus on what the buyer needs to buy. The best relations between salespeople and their customers depend on a solution-driven process, one that involves questioning, listening, and ethically aligning the customer's need with the seller's product.

VARIATION

The concept of reciprocity (as shown in concern for the salesperson's need to sell and the buyer's need or non-need to purchase) represents the yin/yang nature of interpersonal relationships. Thus, it can be used in any number of other training programs. Examples follow.

- *Listening*. Have participants work in pairs. One person speaks for a minute regarding an "easy" topic: hobby, pet, family, vacation. Before the second person can continue the conversation, he or she must paraphrase what was said by the first speaker.

- *Memory Development*. We often forget the names of those to whom we've been introduced because we're concerned about the impression we may be making on the person. To help participants focus on the name as it's spoken, ask the second person in a dialogue to inquire about the name before launching into his or her own introduction.

- *Supervision*. Have new supervisors recall the best and worst experiences they've had working for other supervisors. Then have them explain to their triad partners how they are actively working to incorporate the best into their own supervisory style and what they are doing to actively avoid the worst traits they've encountered.

- *Communication*. Whether it's a letter participants have to write, a presentation they have to make, or a briefing they have to conduct, they should consider the WIIFM ("What's In It For Me?") factor: How will the recipient of the information benefit from the idea being proposed or the product being sold?

DISCUSSION

- What steps can salespeople take to move from ego-centrism to other-centrism?

- How much do you know about your customers or clients?

- How much do they know about you?

- What do you do when you learn a client doesn't really need your product?

QUOTATION
"The first step in learning is confusion."

–John Dewey

POINTS OF INTEREST
Lee Iacocca is regarded by many as the "salesperson of the century." And, it was Lee Iacocca himself who asserted that the best thing you could do for your career is learn to think on your feet.

23. Ethical Salesmanship
Info fo' You

Approximately 45 minutes

OVERVIEW
Participants in this exercise actually write a script for an infomercial describing the product or service their organization provides. A panel of impartial judges reviews the presentations and then awards a special trophy to the winning presenters.

PURPOSE
To encourage full disclosure regarding products or services.

GROUP SIZE
Any size group, divided into subgroups of four or five.

ROOM ARRANGEMENT
If possible, table groups for four or five participants.

MATERIALS
- Flipchart and marking pens
- Token prizes (perhaps used books about sales or blue ribbons) for the winning team

PROCEDURE
1. In advance, select a group of outsiders to serve as a panel of judges. They will assess both the effectiveness of the infomercial and its ability to persuade potential buyers to make a purchase.

2. Ask how many have seen an "infomercial" lately. (You may wish to note the word is a portmanteau—a new-word combination of two existing words: "information" and "commercial.") Elicit specific aspects of such presentations.

3. Explain that this exercise requires teams to consider the product or service their organization offers for sale, use, or consumption. (**Note:** If participants represent several different organizations, they can select one product for the group's consideration. Or, they can attempt to "sell" their city, state, or country to foreigners as a place in which to live and/or do business. In the second scenario, they can assume they represent a local or national Chamber of Commerce.) As they consider their "product," teams should list both the pros and cons associated with it.

139

4. Ask them to write a script for an infomercial and rehearse its delivery. This script will be presented as colleagues sit comfortably in front of the room and exchange both information and commercial commentary. They should incorporate the pros and cons listed earlier. The scripts will last no more than 10 minutes each.

5. As they work, have the panel come into the room and arrange for them to be seated in the back. Ensure they have paper and pencil in case they wish to take notes.

6. Once all the infomercials have been delivered, allow the judges a few minutes to compare notes and then ask them to declare a winner. Invite them to explain the rationale behind their choice and ask how they were affected by the presentation of product pros and cons.

VARIATION
Ask participants to make lists of other portmanteaux that have applications to sales. Use as an example the portmanteau created by former Los Angeles Lakers' coach, Pat Riley, who legally owns the word "three-peat."

DISCUSSION
- How do you as a buyer respond to "truth in advertising"?
- In what ways is an effective salesperson like an effective trial attorney?
- What are both the pros and cons of full disclosure?

QUOTATION
"In the mountains of truth you never climb in vain."
– Friedrich Nietzsche

POINTS OF INTEREST
The potential cost of dishonesty—loss of reputation and loss of customers, to say nothing of lawsuits—heavily outweighs the painful truth. There are, however, ways to be truthful without putting yourself or your product in a negative position. In their classic book on marketing, authors Al Ries and Jack Trout tell the true story of a bank officer named Young J. Boozer. If this were your name, you might honestly go by the initials of Y. J. Boozer or use your middle name instead.

You could avoid the awkward occurrence that took place when a customer called the bank and asked to speak to "Young Boozer." The switchboard operator brightly responded, "We have a lot of them around here. Which one do you want to talk to?"

24. Ethical Salesmanship
Ethics—from A to Z

Approximately 20 minutes

OVERVIEW
This exercise, which works especially well as an energizer, involves a competition of sorts. The first triad to finish listing 26 ethical sales behaviors—each starting with a different letter of the alphabet—wins a token prize.

PURPOSE
To broaden the salesperson's range of successful behaviors.

GROUP SIZE
Any size group, divided into triads.

ROOM ARRANGEMENT
Flexible seating, so participants can easily form triads.

MATERIALS
Optional: Three cans of alphabet soup or three boxes of alphabet cereal.

PROCEDURE
1. Announce that you are challenging the group to an informal competition, but one that will provide much "food for ethical thought."

2. Explain that each triad is to come up with 26 sentences. Each sentence must start with a letter of the alphabet, beginning with an A-verb such as "Ask...." The 26th sentence will be a Z-verb such as "Zero in on...." (It's also permitted to modify a verb and use the modifying word as the first word of the sentence. So, they could write "Zealously guard...." for their Z-verb sentence.)

VARIATION
The A-to-Z competition can be used with any other training program.

DISCUSSION
- What "foolish" thing can you do to increase sales—something that might make you feel foolish for a few minutes but that might pique the interest of a buyer?

- Which of the 26 possibilities are you not yet employing but could employ to increase sales?

- How often do you simply brainstorm ways to increase sales?

QUOTATION
"There is a foolish corner in the brain of the wisest man."
– Aristotle

POINTS OF INTEREST
Harvard Professor Howard Gardner is famous for his studies of the creative personality. His research has led him to realize that creative individuals—from all walks of life—engage in three techniques: they spend time each day reflecting; they refuse to let failure shape their future actions; they capitalize on their strengths.

25. Ethical Salesmanship
Sell-ebrities

Approximately 45 minutes

OVERVIEW
Participants are asked to select a famous celebrity who—if money were no object—could best represent the product or service they sell. Then they are asked to identify the traits associated with that individual and to prepare a short pitch incorporating one of those traits.

PURPOSE
- To specify the qualities associated with widely admired individuals.
- To plan a sales pitch that illustrates some of those qualities.

GROUP SIZE
Any size group, divided into subgroups of four or five.

ROOM ARRANGEMENT
If possible, table groups for four or five participants.

MATERIALS
Small scraps of paper. (Each person receives a number equivalent to the number of groups minus one. If there are 20 people and four groups of five, each person would receive three sheets of paper, making 60 the total number of sheets you'll need.) **Optional:** Possible token prizes for the group with the highest sell-ability.

METHOD
1. Form groups of four or five and ask the group at large how many play golf. Then ask, "Are you more or less likely to buy a product if Tiger Woods is endorsing it?" Continue the opening by asking similar questions: "How many of you admire Michael Jordan?" Then, "Do you buy Hanes underwear because he pitches it?" And, for those with long memories, "How many of you purchased a Mr. Coffee coffee machine because Joe DiMaggio told you that you should?" (Note: Don't limit your examples to all males or to all sports figures.)

2. Discuss the fact that celebrities earn millions of dollars because of these endorsements. Ask how effective participants think such endorsements are.

3. Ask each group to short-list five famous people they'd like selling the product or service their organization provides, and then to prioritize to determine their number one choice.

4. Next, have groups list the attributes they think of when they think about this person. They should like at least three specific traits or behaviors associated with this individual.

5. Ask if (and if so, how often) the word "ethical" appeared in the lists of traits. If it appeared seldom or not at all, ask the group how important ethics is to a salesperson. If it appeared frequently, simply concur in validating its importance.

6. Finally, have groups prepare a short pitch incorporating (or giving evidence of) those specific qualities.

7. Ask each group to appoint one person, who will come forward and deliver the pitch. As he or she comes to the front of the room, place scraps of paper at each table.

8. Following each presentation, ask participants to score the effectiveness of the sales pitch on a scale of 1 to 10, with 10 being highest. Collect the scraps following each group's presentation and add the numbers. Award token prizes or simply your congratulations to the winning team.

9. Let the winners bring closure to the exercise by having them discuss their selections, their final choice, the traits associated with that person, and the way they wove those traits into their sales pitch.

VARIATION

Ask teams of five or six to assume they've been appointed to provide a list of five possible keynote speakers for their next national sales conference. They are to assume money is no object. After 5 or 10 minutes, call on each group to share the lists. Write the names on the flipchart and then ask if anyone notices anything unusual. In all likelihood, the names will primarily be white males. (If not, congratulate the team(s) that supplied the other names.)

Point out the importance of salespeople (managers, leaders, et al.) anticipating criticism that might arise from an honest omission and avoiding charges of sexism or racism or any other "ism" by thinking inclusively.

The exercise, with slight alteration, can also be used in diversity, leadership, and persuasion programs.

When groups have to reduce their lists to one preferred choice (as they do in step 3 of the method), weighted voting might help. With this technique, participants assign weights (think of them as dollars) to the criteria they regard as important in making a selection. Each possible solution or course of action is then evaluated in terms of the degree to which it meets those criteria. The weights are multiplied by the degree to which the choice meets a given criterion. The item with the highest score is the one the team decides to pursue. A simpler variation involves giving each team member three adhesive dots with a number on each. (The number "3" carries the most weight; "2" less; and "1" the least.) Team members stick their "votes" on their prioritized choices, listed on a flipchart. The numbers are then added and the choice with the highest total is the one the group agrees on.

DISCUSSION

- What national or international figure, alive or dead, could persuade you to purchase something you really did not need?

- Analyze the rationale that explains why youngsters *must* have certain celebrity-endorsed products.

- How successful are advertisements that deliberately mismatch appeals—such as having Robert Dole and Britney Spears in the same ad?

QUOTATION

"The two most engaging powers of an author [and possibly of a salesperson as well] are to make new things familiar and familiar things new."

– Samuel Johnson

POINTS OF INTEREST

There are some qualities, like trustworthiness, that separate celebrities from "sell-ebrities." Trustworthiness is a trait you may possess even though your customers or prospective buyers do not know it. One way to demonstrate that customers can count on you to deal honestly is to anticipate objections and address them before the prospect can. In so doing, you show you have nothing to hide. Plus, you have a chance to explain why the good points of your product or service far exceed the negative the prospect might bring up.

26. Ethical Salesmanship
News-Capers

Approximately 40 minutes

OVERVIEW
Participants receive newspapers and pull from them articles illustrating why consumer confidence is eroding. Using those same reasons, participants undertake a Janusian approach to persuade buyers to purchase their product or service.

PURPOSE
To encourage thinking about what does and what does not constitute the organization's values.

GROUP SIZE
Any size group, divided into subgroups of four or five.

ROOM ARRANGEMENT
If possible, table groups for four or five participants.

MATERIALS
Copies of newspapers—they need not be current—so that each person has at least one section (preferably business or current events).

METHOD
1. Begin the exercise by asking if anyone has read about or seen a report such as the "fleecing of America" on the evening news—a report of a shoddy product or a manufacturing recall or an outright transgression of consumers' faith in a given industry or commodity or institution. If not, have a few of your own ready. (On any given day, you are likely to find headlines like the following: "Pentagon disclosures point to misconduct by brass in 13 states"; $10M largest civil penalty against public company over financial reporting"; "Agent: FAA buried lapses"; "Monsanto guilty in Alabama pollution case."

2. Newspaper sections—one for each participant. Allow at least 10 minutes for table groups to list headlines that deal with wrongdoing.

3. Next, ask the table groups to think in reverse terms. How could they take some of these negatives and use their opposites to assure their consumers that the products or services they provide have quality and value. Further, how could they assure their clients that the misdeeds participants have read about would not be tolerated in participants' organizations? (If the groups are composed of

147

individuals representing several different organizations, they can select one to serve as the exemplar.)

4. Ask each group to make a brief presentation about one news report that showed an organization violating some ethical code. Then, ask the group to explain how they converted a negative into a positive selling point for their own product or service.

VARIATION

The concept of Janusian thinking dates back thousands of years to the ancient Romans, who featured this god's head with two profiles on their coins. One profile looked back to the year just ended. The other looked forward to the year about to begin. (The month of January is named after Janus.) The idea of viewing a given situation from opposite perspectives can be applied to courses dealing with Critical Thinking, Problem-Solving, Strategic Planning, and Creativity.

DISCUSSION

- How can an individual or organization that engaged in unethical acts recapture the public's confidence?

- What examples can you recall, from your own private or professional experience, of an organization that acted admirably to make amends for an egregious error?

- What executive-level transgression or decision would cause you to resign from your own organization?

QUOTATION

"There is no fire like passion, there is no shark like hatred, there is no snare like folly, there is no torrent like greed."

– Buddha

POINTS OF INTEREST

In its second annual listing of the "101 Dumbest Moments in Business," *Business 2.0* awards its dubious distinction first of all to Enron for assuming its aggressive accounting cover-ups would never be noticed. Also cited is overseer Arthur Andersen, whose auditors apparently failed to discover the erroneous addition of $1 billion to Enron's assets. Apart from this mega-scandal, what other nominations would you make to next year's list of dumbest business moments?

27. Ethical Salesmanship
Inside Scoops

Approximately 30 minutes

OVERVIEW
The negative fallout from keeping customers "out of the loop" has created glaringly critical outcries from the public. Witness the recent scandals involving cars and tires that were sold despite the companies' knowledge of dangerous deficiencies or medical offices that fail to tell patients their doctors have been convicted of malpractice in other states. Participants in this exercise are asked to consider what customers want to/need to/deserve to/should/shouldn't know about the product or service participants provide.

PURPOSE
To stimulate thinking about the kind of information that can be/should be shared with customers without jeopardizing organizational policies.

GROUP SIZE
Any size group, divided into subgroups of four or five.

ROOM ARRANGEMENT
Seating flexible enough to accommodate groups of different sizes.

MATERIALS
- Handout 27.1, *"Information: Inside/Out"*
- Small scraps of paper

METHOD
1. Elicit examples of organizations that make their customers feel included and/or important by sharing "insider" information—delivery companies, for example, that allow the customer access to tracking information so that they can learn the transit-status of their packages.

2. Ask participants to write a number from 1 to 5 on a scrap of paper. The number indicates the degree to which their own organizations share information with customers: "1" indicates very little "insider" information is shared; "5" indicates the company is exemplary in sharing information with customers.

3. Form groups on the basis of the numbers—all the "1"s will sit together; all the "2"s will sit together, et cetera. Have them briefly discuss why they assigned the numbers they did.

4. Distribute Handout 27.1 and allow 10 to 15 minutes for completion. (**Note:** If participants are not all from the same organization, have the subgroups select one representative organization to use in their handout-matrix.)

5. Conclude the exercise by having one group sit in a "fishbowl" with the other participants seated around the inner circle. Have the fishbowl-group explain their decisions while the others assume the role of customers.

6. Wrap up by having the "customers" provide feedback on the report they heard from the fishbowl-group.

VARIATION
Consider using a focus group to learn how customers feel/would feel about certain information-sharing changes your sales team may be considering.

1. Assemble a group of six or seven representative customers.

2. Advise them that you'd like to tape record or videotape their meeting.

3. Create a relaxed atmosphere within a structured (agenda-driven) framework and with a moderator who can refrain from becoming involved in the responses to the questions he or she poses.

4. Have the sales team in the background, taking notes on their observations but not participating in any way in the discussion.

5. The sales team should meet as soon as possible following the focus group meeting, with the original problem-solvers/decision-makers. They should evaluate their impressions and compare them to the actual tape recording. Focus-group input is one valuable means of determining what customers would like to know and what they feel they need to know.

DISCUSSION
- What information is "closely held" in your own organization?
- Does your organization have its secrets?
- Does the withholding of this information from consumers cross any ethical barriers?
- What information not now provided to customers do you feel they would appreciate having?

QUOTATION
"The man who is denied the opportunity of making decisions of importance begins to regard as important the decisions he is allowed to make."

– C. Northcote Parkinson

POINTS OF INTEREST

In keeping with the Quality movement's definitions of "internal customers" (those who receive the output of our work) and "external customers" (those who purchase the actual product or service provided by the organization), you can extend the need-to-know idea to a Supervision class or a class dealing with Interviews or Hiring and Firing.

An important distinction supervisors need to make is that between disability and inability. According to the *Supervisor's Guide to Employment Practices*, an employee who cannot read because of dyslexia is covered under the American with Disabilities Act (ADA) and, in all likelihood, will have to be accommodated on the job. On the other hand, someone who cannot read because he or she never completed school may have an "inability" rather than a "disability" and, therefore, may not be covered.

Basically, the act states companies cannot discriminate against individuals with disabilities who are otherwise qualified to perform the basic functions of the job. Reasonable accommodations must be made to allow such individuals to do their job.

The difficulty in many cases, of course, is in the acquisition of the information you need. Extreme sensitivity will be required to learn what you need to know.

Handout 27.1
Information: Inside/Out

1. What is the primary product or service your organization provides?

2. What are the ten most significant facts regarding that product or service?

3. How many of these does your average customer know about?

4. Complete the following matrix with reference to information about your product or service. Keep in mind these questions as you do so:

    ✓ If customers were to come in and examine our books, would they find anything that would embarrass us? Does any of the information we are not sharing constitute legal, moral, or ethical violations?

    ✓ If I were a consumer of this product or a user of the service we provide, what do I know as an insider that I would want to know as an outsider?

    ✓ Is this information being shared with the public? Why or why not?

    ✓ Is there ever a rationale for "full disclosure"? Why or why not?

    ✓ What are the pros and cons of sharing internal information with outsiders?

Fill in the four quadrants below in relation to the product or service your organization provides. Then determine how much of that information is currently being shared.

Information that the public…

Would regard as nice to know	Would find necessary to know
Deserves to know	Would not regard as necessary

28. Ethical Salesmanship
Ethics Audit

Approximately 25 minutes

OVERVIEW
This exercise affords participants an opportunity to assess their sales culture via an ethics audit. The audit follows a brief discussion of the extent to which those at the top influence that culture.

PURPOSE
To generate discussion regarding elements of the organizational culture that may need strengthening.

GROUP SIZE
Any size group.

ROOM ARRANGEMENT
No special arrangements required.

MATERIALS
Handout 28.1, *"Culture Audit"*

PROCEDURE
1. Point out that the current spate of corporate scandals has roots that extend deep into the soil of immorality and illegality. Supply a few examples, such as the 1991 Wall Street scandal that found Salomon Brothers' CEO remaining silent for four months after he was made aware that his stock exchange traders had acted improperly in bidding on Treasury securities. (One employee explained away the impropriety as a "practical joke"—a joke the security regulators didn't find funny.) His silence cost CEO John Gutfreund his job.

2. Lead a brief discussion concerning the extent to which the culture's tone is established by those at the top—those with sufficient clout to influence the buying and selling patterns of thousands of others.

3. Distribute Handout 28.1 and have participants work on it individually. Have small groups discuss their most extreme replies.

VARIATION

Ask for a volunteer to distribute the survey organization-wide (with some word-smithing to make it applicable to any employee), after obtaining the necessary approvals, and to analyze the results. (Professional courtesy dictates the analysis be shared with senior management before it is distributed throughout the organization.)

Have participants develop their own assessment tools with statements that require an analysis of existing procedures/practices/philosophies. Have them indicate where ethical lines are being crossed, thus creating potentially serious consequences for the individual (and his or her job), the team, the department, and even the organization. Have participants compare their assessments and—if several participants work in the same department—create a synthesized tool that can be taken back to the workplace and used to create/enforce ethical policies.

DISCUSSION

What drives people to remain silent despite their knowledge of wrongdoing? What is/should be your organization's procedure for whistleblowers to follow? What ethical tone is being set in your own organization by those in authority?

QUOTATION

"If we could read the secret history of our enemies, we should find in each man's life, sorrow and suffering enough to disarm all hostility."

– Henry Wadsworth Longfellow

POINTS OF INTEREST

Speaking of the need to rid the whole culture of unethical practices and not just isolate a small number of people or practices, management consultant Frank J. Navran uses the metaphor of a "flea dip." He likens the elimination of a particular ethical problem to a flea dip—which will remove fleas from your pet… until it returns to its everyday environment. There, in all likelihood, the animal will pick up fleas once again.

Navran maintains the establishment of an ethical environment depends on two things:

✓ Putting the right people in the right place.

✓ Rewarding the people who are behind the change efforts.

Handout 28.1
Culture Audit

Directions
Circle the number that comes closest to the description you feel best applies to your organization.

Sales Environment

1. Relationship between sales manager and staff is:

   Demeaning, impersonal   1 2 3 4 5 6 7 8 9 10   **Encouraging, supportive**

2. Top decision-makers:

   Place equal weight on profit and values   1 2 3 4 5 6 7 8 9 10   **Are profit-driven above all else**

3. Organizational leaders:

   Reflect poorly on the firm's integrity   1 2 3 4 5 6 7 8 9 10   **Make us proud to be working in this firm**

4. Advertising for our products is:

   Negative; focused on sex or violence   1 2 3 4 5 6 7 8 9 10   **Fun, wholesome, honest**

5. Relationships among sales staff can be described as:

   Dog-eat-dog; secretive; highly competitive   1 2 3 4 5 6 7 8 9 10   **Sharing; cooperative; harmonious**

Ethical Environment

6. Customers:

| Are misled, taken advantage of | 1 2 3 4 5 6 7 8 9 10 | Are given a fair deal |

7. Vendors are viewed as:

| A source of irritation | 1 2 3 4 5 6 7 8 9 10 | Partners in the manufacturing/ sales process |

8. The product or service we provide is:

| Not one I'd recommend to my family | 1 2 3 4 5 6 7 8 9 10 | Among the best you can find anywhere |

9. Competitors are:

| Badmouthed, mocked to customers | 1 2 3 4 5 6 7 8 9 10 | Referred to and treated respectfully |

10. In sales meetings:

| Agendas are hidden | 1 2 3 4 5 6 7 8 9 10 | Issues are dealt with honestly and openly |

Handout 28.1: *Culture Audit* (concluded)

Interpretation:

If your score is less than 50, there's a good possibility your organization is consumed by the profit factor. While this is not necessarily a bad thing, if the drive toward profit reaches greed-levels, it can dominate the decisions being made and actions being taken. It's also possible that your score reflects dissatisfaction with either the company you've chosen to work for or your chosen profession itself. To further ascertain if the dissatisfaction your score reflects is widely held, make a copy of the culture assessment and ask at least five colleagues to fill it out. Compare your answers with theirs.

If you scored from 50 to 70, your organization could probably be regarded as average in terms of the value it places on values themselves. There's room for improvement here. Consider ways to effect that improvement.

A score of 71 to 89 reflects a company that probably won't make the list of Top 100 Companies to Work for in America. Nonetheless, all the right ingredients are here for a culture of ethical success. Refinement is called for in some areas but, in all likelihood, there are no glaring gaps between what's right and what's being done.

Your firm, if you rated it 90 or above, might easily qualify for that Top 100 list. It would appear you are proud of your association with this organization and with the product or service it offers customers. As good as the organization is, though, a commitment to continuous improvement will keep it good and, perhaps, make it outstanding. Remember the Lexus ad: "The relentless pursuit of perfection."

Reproduced from *50 Reproducible Activities for Promoting Ethics Within the Organization*, by Marlene Caroselli. HRD Press, 2015.

29. Ethical Salesmanship
Take the "Ow" Out of "Now"

Approximately 20 minutes

OVERVIEW
"Now" is one of the words to which potential buyers are most likely to respond. Participants in this exercise are tasked with identifying key words that attract customers. They are also shown a list of persuasive words. Then, they are given a product for which to prepare an advertisement that uses some of these words in an ethical fashion and one that does just the opposite.

PURPOSE
To provide participants with a list of words that can be used to describe a product or service.

GROUP SIZE
Any size group, divided into an even number of subgroups.

ROOM ARRANGEMENT
Two, four, or six table groups of three to six participants each.

MATERIALS
- Flipchart and marking pens
- Equipment for displaying PowerPoint slides
- Slide 29.1, *"Words That Work"*
- Handout 29.1, *"Article: 'Your' Key to Closing More Sales"*

PROCEDURE
1. Begin with a discussion of "trigger words," both positive and negative, that influence participants as buyers, as employees, and as members of a diverse society.

2. Write these words on a flipchart sheet that has two columns: one for the positive words and one for the negative.

3. Next, discuss the ethics of using certain words. Note the political campaigns that successfully employ negatives. Then note the positive words that have proven successful in swaying consumers to actually make a purchase. One of them is the word "now." Point out there's an "ow" factor in such words—if a false sense of urgency is created, if consumers are manipulated into making a decision before they've had sufficient time to consider it, using the word "now" could subject the seller to claims of unethical behavior.

161

4. Display Slide 29.1, *"Words That Work,"* which contains persuasive words. Divide the group into an even number of subgroups. (Each subgroup, ideally, will have the same number of participants.)

5. Explain that half the subgroups will be asked to develop an ad (using at least three words on the list or on the flipchart) that makes an ethical appeal to potential buyers. The other half of the subgroups will create an ad using at least three words from the list on the slide or the flipchart list. Their ad will make an unethical or manipulative appeal to potential buyers.

6. Place some object in the room or on your person (a wallet, a watch, a pen) in a prominent position and allow the groups about 15 minutes to create their ads trying to sell that object.

VARIATION
Invite, if possible, the head of the sales department to select the ad he or she feels is most persuasive. Discuss the use, misuse, and abuse of words from an ethical perspective, using that person's selection as a starting point.

Distribute Handout 29.1, the article on guerrilla selling, *"'Your' Key to Closing More Sales,"* by Don Cooper, and discuss the points made.

DISCUSSION
- How sophisticated do you feel the average consumer is?
- What prompts you to make the purchases you make?
- What phrases turn you off? Why?

QUOTATION
"The simple act of paying attention can take you a long way."
– Keanu Reeves

POINTS OF INTEREST
John R. Graham, president of Graham Communications in Quincy, Massachusetts, heads a marketing services and sales consulting firm. He advises clients to eliminate negative statements or those that may create an impression that is negative. For example, saying, "They didn't get back to me" suggests you are not willing to take the initiative to find out what you or a client needs to know. Consider the negative implications associated with the following phrases:

- ✓ "I thought someone else was taking care of that."
- ✓ "I didn't know you wanted me to do that."
- ✓ "I didn't think about that."
- ✓ "As I understand it… "
- ✓ "I've been trying to get everyone together, but…"

Slide 29.1

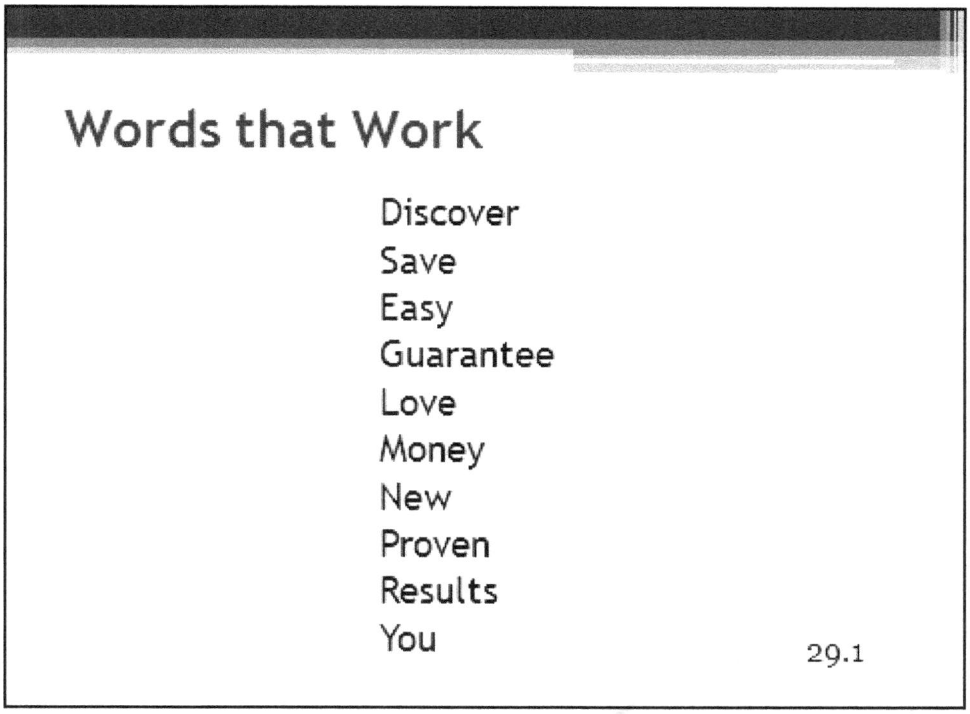
Words that Work
Discover
Save
Easy
Guarantee
Love
Money
New
Proven
Results
You
29.1

Handout 29.1
Article: *"Your" Key to Closing More Sales*
By Don Cooper

One of the most powerful words in a salesperson's verbal arsenal is "your." While most salespeople focus on "our products," "our services," and "the history of our company," top sales performers prefer to talk about "your needs," "your experiences," and "your results."

As a customer, you don't think about the salesperson, their product, or their commission. You think about how the product or service might solve your problem. You think about your budget and your priorities. You think about how the product makes you feel. Savvy salespeople tap into those thoughts and emotions by using the word "your" liberally in their questioning and in their presentation.

Here's how one sales pro, Dana Stephenson of San Diego Harley-Davidson, uses this tactic to sell more to her customers: "As soon as a person tries on a piece of clothing, I start referring to it as 'yours.' I say things like, 'Let me see how your shirt looks.' 'Would you like me to hold your jacket while you try on these other items?' and 'Do you have the shoes to complete your outfit?'"

As Dana noted, "When you refer to something as 'your' item, in the customer's mind, they already own it. So they stop thinking about whether or not they want to buy it. The sale is already closed."

Reprinted with permission from   Don Cooper
2802 Sundown Lane, #203
Boulder, Colorado 80303

Don Cooper—"America's Networking Guru"—is a sales and marketing expert who speaks, writes, and consults on how to attract and keep more customers. He is a contributing author of Confessions of Shameless Self Promoters *with Debbie Allen and Jay Conrad Levinson. You can contact Don by phone at 303-449-1389 or 303-885-1182 or by e-mail at Don@DonCooper.com. You can also find other articles at www.DonCooper.com.*

Reproduced from *50 Reproducible Activities for Promoting Ethics Within the Organization*, by Marlene Caroselli. HRD Press, 2015.

30. Ethical Salesmanship
Drug Testing: An Employer's Right or an Employee's Wrong?

Approximately 25 minutes

OVERVIEW

The question of testing for drugs has spread from the workplace to the schoolroom, with vocal and angry proponents on each side of the issue. With this exercise, participants have an opportunity to view two possible interpretations of any given action before determining whether or not to discuss the delicate issue of drugs with a newly hired salesperson.

PURPOSE

- To point out the potential danger of making accusatory statements.
- To provide assistance in making determinations regarding a drug policy.

GROUP SIZE

Any size group, divided into subgroups of four or five.

ROOM ARRANGEMENT

Any kind of seating will work, as participants will work in pairs.

MATERIALS

Handout 30.1, *"Naturally High?"*

PROCEDURE

1. Solicit participants' views about the current drug problem in America and the depths to which it is sinking: the evening news on April 13, 2002, reported a 12-year-old child working as a "drug mule." Ask if the concept of a "drug-free America" is more dream than possibility. Talk about the Drug-free Workplace Act that mandates the implementation of a drug abuse prevention program for all private-sector companies that serve as vendors to the federal government.

2. Ask participants not to mention names of individuals or companies as they reply to the following question: Have you ever worked with a person who you suspected was on drugs? Discuss the potential hazards of such a person's actions.

3. Distribute Handout 30.1, *"Naturally High?"* Explain that the exercise they're about to work on involves a salesperson suspected of being on drugs. They'll work with a partner on the case study.

167

4. After approximately 15 minutes, ask for volunteers to tell what they would have done in this scenario and why.

5. Conclude with a discussion of the services being provided by the organization's Human Resources Department. If participants are unaware of such services, discuss the elements that should make up a policy regarding substance abuse in the workplace.

VARIATION

Develop role-plays that deal with a number of delicate issues: possible drug use, theft, alcoholism, rumor-mongering. Divide the class into triads and have one person serve as the suspected violator, a second the concerned co-worker or supervisor, and a third person the observer who will provide feedback to both parties.

Invite a member of the Human Resources Department to address the group regarding existing policies and services.

DISCUSSION

- Do you feel drug testing in the workplace and in the schools violates civil rights?

- Extend this observation: "Alcohol is not about thirst. Obesity is not about hunger." If there's truth to these assertions, then what is drug addiction about?

- What must you think about before making an accusation regarding drugs or theft or any other illegal or immoral behavior?

QUOTATION

"Never bear more than one trouble at a time. Some people bear three kinds—all they have had, all they have now, and all they expect to have."

– Edward Everett Hale

POINTS OF INTEREST

The Supervisor's Guide to Employment Practices provides these symptoms associated with various drugs:

Marijuana	Fatigue; dry, irritated coughing; sore throat; red eyes, dilated pupils
Cocaine	Irritability; decreased attention span; restlessness; paranoia; hallucinations; increased blood pressure and heart rate; blurred vision; muscle tension and tremors; slurred speech; thirst; excessive perspiration; dizziness; headaches; nausea; diarrhea
Opiates	Drowsiness; constipation; nausea and vomiting; constricted pupils; depression; apathy; lethargy; watery eyes; muscle cramps; loss of appetite
Phencyclidine (PCP or Angel Dust)	Lack of coordination; confusion; agitation; severe mood swings; erratic and violent behavior
Amphetamines	Hyperexcitability; restlessness; talkativeness; insomnia; violence; nausea; vomiting; diarrhea; cramps; headaches; hypertension; pallor; palpitations

Handout 30.1
Naturally High?

Case Study

John Smith is a relatively new salesperson in an educational services company. He was hired to sell seminars to accountants, attorneys, business owners, and Human Resource professionals. Although he seems naturally exuberant, of late his fellow salespeople and his boss have noticed a change in his behavior. He's experiencing mood swings. Further, he often seems confused and easily agitated.

Questions

1. What, if anything, would you do if you were John's co-worker or boss? Other than drugs, what other possible causes might explain the changes in John's behavior?

2. What symptoms do you usually associate with someone who is on drugs?

3. Which of those symptoms have you experienced yourself?

4. If you choose to speak with John about what you've observed, what would your exact words be?

5. How far should a person's right to privacy extend?

6. If John's sales record is as high as ever, would you intervene? Explain.

7. If his sales plummet, would you intervene? Explain.

Reproduced from *50 Reproducible Activities for Promoting Ethics Within the Organization*, by Marlene Caroselli. HRD Press, 2015.

Part D:
Ethical Management
Introduction: Nan DeMars

The Manager's Responsibility for the Ethical Office

Robert MacGregor, former president of the Minnesota Center for Corporate Responsibility, told me once he has the same discussion with every assistant he has ever hired. On the first day of the job, he tells them: *"I'm going to be going 100 miles per hour. You will be going 120 miles per hour to stay ahead of me. In my haste to get a job done by deadline, if I ever appear to be cutting corners or sliding into unethical practices in any regard, I WANT you to stop me. It is YOUR responsibility to keep me on the ethical track. In other words, I want you to be my ethical monitor."*

That's my dream! If every manager would have that conversation with every employee he or she supervises, we would be well underway to establishing and maintaining The Ethical Office.

The Ethical Office is a *culture that fosters mutual respect, trust, and honest communication among co-workers, customers, and vendors.* The concept is becoming another means for achieving competitive advantage, as companies increasingly see the link between healthy profits and ethical cultures.

As a result, organizations today are:

- Writing extensive codes of ethics/conduct

- Expanding employee handbooks for guidelines

- Incorporating ethics training (with discussions of reality-based case studies)

- Creating ethics hotlines (often anonymous)

- Hiring ethics directors

- Establishing ethics departments or appointing a human resource representative "point person" whom employees can approach with ethical dilemmas

This aggressive approach to championing The Ethical Workplace is paying off in the following high dividends:

- *Productivity* – Ethical employees outperform all others. They sell more products, receive fewer service calls, and post superior profit margins. The "personality" of an ethical office is healthy, energized, forward-looking, confident, creative, and resourceful. It's a real "can-do" place to work because people are not confused about what is expected of them, nor are they stressed to distraction.

- *Accountability* – With a clear understanding of what is expected of them, employees take responsibility and feel accountable for their personal behavior and performance, regardless of their position. They take responsibility to resolve ethical dilemmas. They place high value on personal integrity.

- *Communication* –Employees *want* to talk about ethical dilemmas as they arise. The manager who encourages this open communication will enjoy earlier resolution of problems and less confusion (two cost-saving advantages).

- *Confidentiality* – Information is power, and the unethical office has zero confidentiality. Managers should emphasize the importance of erring on the safe side and treating everything as confidential unless told otherwise. Instilling this respect for the confidential office will result in buttoned-up information about deadlines, prices, budgets, performance reviews, and product services. Everyone wins here.

- *Stability* – Employees *stay* in an ethical atmosphere, and that is cost-saving in itself. The unethical office results in a revolving door in the human resource department. And the costs associated with the departure of disgruntled employees along with the resulting hiring of new employees are always high.

- *Predictability* –The Ethical Office avoids being blindsided by surprises such as harassment lawsuits and compromised security. In an ethical culture, employees address ethical dilemmas as they surface and nip them in the bud before they get out of hand.

Employees *want* to do the right thing—and they also want to trust the people they work with every day. It is the manager's responsibility to create the safe atmosphere of an Ethical Workplace for their employees. The rewards will be overwhelming.

Submitted by: Nan DeMars
                    Executary Services
                    7424 Cahill Road
                    Minneapolis, Minnesota 55439
                    Phone: 612-835-1148
                    Fax: 612-831-7908
                    E-mail: DearNan@office-ethics.com
                    Web site: www.office-ethics.com

Nan DeMars is an office ethics trainer/consultant and author of *You Want Me To Do **What?*** (Simon & Schuster). She conducts training throughout the United States and in foreign countries. In addition, she is president of Executary Services, a seminar/search/office ethics consultant firm in Minneapolis.

31. Ethical Management
Ethics Evaluation

Approximately 60 minutes (longer if there are more than three subgroups)

OVERVIEW
Many companies have written policies on ethics that are distributed on paper or are available on an Intranet. In this exercise, leaders and managers are able to sharpen their awareness and understanding of the policy by "playing" with it in a learning situation.

PURPOSE
To enable participants to learn what the official ethics policy means to them and how they and colleagues would contribute to enforcing that policy.

GROUP SIZE
Any size group, divided into subgroups of four or five.

ROOM ARRANGEMENT
Flexible seating to permit table groups of four or five.

MATERIALS
- Handout 31.1, *"Directions"*
- Flipchart and marking pens
- Copies of the ethics policy being considered. (**Note:** If participants represent several different organizations, select one representative policy.)

PROCEDURE
1. Introduce the purpose and method of the exercise to the group. Lead a brief discussion of the importance of having such a policy and having it well publicized in the organization.

2. Distribute written copies of the ethics policy to be used in the exercise and allow sufficient time for people to read it.

3. Divide the group into subgroups of four or five participants.

4. Give each group the copies of Handout 30.1, *"Directions."* Allow at least 30 minutes for completion.

5. Bring the subgroups back together and let each in turn present their findings.

6. Highlight the differences in the way the policy is interpreted and in the way it is applied.

7. Lead a discussion on whether these differences are acceptable.

8. Ask for suggestions to improve the clarity of the policy and the guidelines for applying it.

9. Ask for volunteers who are willing to pass on these suggestions to the policy-makers.

10. Wrap up by discussing ways the ethics policy can be more fully utilized and applied. Discuss, too, the "courage" shown by those volunteers willing to speak with senior management regarding improvements to the ethics policy.

VARIATION

Have subgroups prepare an ideal ethics policy. Have them exchange and critique each other's policy.

Take a macrocosmic perspective: Ask subgroups to prepare an ethics policy for the industry as a whole or for political leaders, educational leaders, religious leaders, et cetera.

DISCUSSION

- What forces might have influenced the originators of the organizational policy being studied?
- How often should such a policy be re-visited/revised?
- Should the policy reflect input from every organizational level?
- If so, how could that input be obtained and incorporated?
- Should the policy reflect input from those outside the organization?
- If so, what particular groups should be invited to contribute their thoughts?

QUOTATION

"Everyone is a genius at least once a year."

– Georg Christoph Lichtenberg

POINTS OF INTEREST

Authors Michael Beer and Russell Eisenstat have identified six "silent killers" related to strategy implementation. Too many managers, they maintain, avoid confronting these killers. Relate these to the successful implementation of an ethics-policy implementation.

- ✓ Top-down or laissez-faire senior management style
- ✓ Unclear strategy and conflict priorities
- ✓ Ineffective senior management team
- ✓ Poor vertical communication
- ✓ Poor coordination across functions, businesses, or borders
- ✓ Inadequate down-the-line leadership skills and development

Handout 31.1
Directions

Directions

1. Review the written policy and identify the parts that are clear to you and the parts that are less clear.

2. Describe what you are responsible for with regard to this policy.

3. Describe how you (or others) ensure that the policy is understood by employees.

4. Give one or two examples of situations in your day-to-day work in which this policy is especially applicable or relevant.

5. For each example, describe how you or others monitor whether the policy is being applied.

6. For each example, describe what your actions would be if you found out the policy was being violated.

7. Note the differences among the members of your group with regard to points 1 through 6.

8. Present your results at the plenary session.

Submitted by: Mike Morrell, Senior Consultant,
Organizational and Staff Development
AtosOriginCOPM
Postbox 218
5600 MD Eindhoven
The Netherlands
Telephone: +31(0)6 – 53 17 50 71
E-mail: mikemorrell@atosorigin.com

Mike enjoys the process of discovering what it means to be a human being. He sees organizations and organizational development as the product of—and the current environment for—the further development of and interplay between individuals. He facilitates both organizational and individual staff development in the roles of trainer, coach, consultant, and change manager.

Reproduced from *50 Reproducible Activities for Promoting Ethics Within the Organization*,
by Marlene Caroselli. HRD Press, 2015.

32. Ethical Management
Rites, Rights, and Wrongs

Approximately 30 minutes

OVERVIEW
The focus of this exercise is the delicate balance between one's right to act as he or she wishes and the effects those individual actions can have on others. Participants are asked to prepare a script that has one employee suggesting to another that he or she may need to "tone down" his or her remarks a bit.

PURPOSE
To explore the issue of individual rights and the boundaries that may be crossed in the exercise of those rights.

GROUP SIZE
Any size group can participate in this exercise.

ROOM ARRANGEMENT
Seating flexible enough to accommodate a fishbowl arrangement with one small group on the inside and a ring of observers circling them. (**Note:** If the class size is greater than fifteen, have two fishbowls concurrently.)

MATERIALS
Handout 32.1, *"Chestnuts Roasting"*

METHOD
1. Begin with a discussion of "rites" and "rights." One rite might be the initiation rituals that encourage excessive drinking. While a 21-year-old has the right to drink as much as he chooses, a moral question arises: Is it right for his fraternity brothers to encourage excesses that could be injurious, if not fatal? Another rite in which sports-loving Americans engage is the celebration following the winning of a national championship. To be sure, we have the right to celebrate. Invariably, it seems that right is eventually accompanied by destruction of property as well as legal, moral, and ethical rules. Another example would be the right of a woman to determine what happens to her body. Some would argue she loses that right, though, if it means the death of an unborn child.

2. Distribute Handout 32.1, *"Chestnuts Roasting,"* and have triads work on it for 15 to 20 minutes.

181

3. Ask one triad to sit in the center of the room while the other participants sit on the outside of the "fishbowl" and take notes on the proceedings.

4. Debrief by asking for input from the observers regarding the effectiveness of the script in respecting one person's rights without infringing on the right of all persons in a workplace to be treated respectfully.

VARIATION

- Ask each triad for the one line they felt would be most effective in circumstances such as these. Record the lines on a flipchart and encourage participants to make note of them and to use them in the future.

- Although the telling of "war stories" can be a waste of instructional time, if the contributions are guided, many valuable lessons can be learned. Have triads discuss some of the worst things that have ever been said to them by a manager—statements that may have been unethical, illegal, or perhaps simply hurtful. Have them vote on the most horrific horror story and ask each triad to tell that story in less than 3 minutes. (Warn them in advance that you may have to interrupt to get to the point.)

DISCUSSION

- What examples can you cite of a rite or right that, if carried to an extreme, can become a wrong?

- What civil rights do you feel are being/have been abrogated in America today?

- If you were to champion a cause, what would it be?

- Are there rights that others opposed to your cause would say you are violating?

QUOTATION

"In the world that is coming, if you can't navigate differences, you've had it."
– Robert Hughes

POINTS OF INTEREST

As reported in the *Democrat and Chronicle*, mega-mogul Ted Turner addressed students at Harvard Law School in April 2001. His topic: *"Our Common Future."* His remarks included these:

- ✓ "But, you know, communism is an endangered species."

- ✓ "When I offend people, I apologize. I've apologized to just about every group around. I'll even apologize to you."

as well as a defense of these earlier remarks:

- ✓ "Christianity is a religion for losers."
- ✓ "The pope is an idiot."
- ✓ "The U.S. has some of the dumbest people in the world."
- ✓ "Fidel Castro is a hell of a guy."
- ✓ "The First Commandment is obsolete."

Discuss the ethical overtones of such remarks. Then, juxtapose them with the facts that:

- ✓ As the nation's largest single landowner, he has pledged that his 1.7 million acres will be preserved in their natural state in perpetuity.
- ✓ The Turner Foundation gives $50 million annually for environmental activities.
- ✓ In 1997, he contributed $1 billion to programs connected with the United Nations.
- ✓ He has donated $250 million to his newly formed Nuclear Threat Initiative, dedicated to safely disposing of nuclear waste material and stopping the spread of nuclear and biological weapons.

Handout 32.1
Chestnuts Roasting

Case Study

Vincent Arturo is an immensely likeable fellow. There is no pretense about him. He tends to say what's on his mind—without artifice and, sometimes, without forethought. Because he founded and continues to sponsor a mentoring program in the organization, he's been asked to address the "Ceiling-Smashers," a women's group within the organization, dedicated to the advancement of women and minorities.

You attended the conference and cringed when he made these remarks:

> *"I want to acknowledge my secretary, Sue. She's that pretty little thing sitting in the front row. And yes, she's had to pull my chestnuts out of the fire on more than one occasion."*

> *"Spaghetti-spinners like me know the importance of family support."*

> *"I see none of you are barefoot and only two of you are pregnant. Good. That means you're making progress."*

As Vincent's manager, you've decided to speak with him regarding his remarks. While you're certain he meant no one any harm, you're equally certain others took offense—having seen and heard the reactions of the audience. Prepare a script with your team, showing what you would say as a manager and what Vincent's likely response would be. (Remember, the purpose behind every managerial chat of this nature is to effect improvement.)

Reproduced from *50 Reproducible Activities for Promoting Ethics Within the Organization*, by Marlene Caroselli. HRD Press, 2015.

33. Ethical Management
That Feather in Your Cap

Approximately 35 minutes

OVERVIEW

The case study in this exercise helps participants explore the ethical issues associated with credit earned and credit due. Trust, ethics, credibility, and reliability are some matters addressed in this exercise.

PURPOSE

- To encourage thought and discussion regarding instances when it may be necessary to challenge management's position.
- To develop positive approaches for handling this type of situation.

GROUP SIZE

Any size group, divided into subgroups of four or five.

ROOM ARRANGEMENT

If possible, table groups for four or five participants.

MATERIALS

Handout 33.1, *"Case Study"*

PROCEDURE

1. Ask participants how they would interpret this statement, one that a government employee says he would like to deliver to his supervisor one day: "That feather in your cap came out of my tail!"

2. Discuss possible reasons to explain why some supervisors take credit that isn't rightfully theirs and why others are more inclined to acknowledge their employees' contributions.

3. Distribute Handout 33.1, *Case Study,* depicting a real-world scenario and ask table groups to discuss the related questions.

4. Upon conclusion of the discussion, begin a flipchart list of "10 Commanagements"—"commandments" that supervisors/managers would ideally follow to create the best of all management worlds. Call on one spokesperson from each group to contribute one recommendation, stated as a "should" or "should not" sentence related to valuing employees' contributions.

VARIATION
Compile several lists of "Commanagements"—related to various issues that arise during the course of a program. Encourage participants to compile these lists with co-workers upon their return to the workplace.

DISCUSSION
- What prompts some supervisors to steal credit from others?

- How can you relate Dr. W. Edwards Deming's insistence on "driving out fear" to events in the workplace?

- Jack Welch, former CEO of General Electric, often speaks about confidence. Explore the effects—both positive and negative—of confidence and a lack of confidence.

QUOTATION
"An invasion of armies can be resisted, but not an idea whose time has come."
                                                            – Victor Hugo

POINTS OF INTEREST
In *The Power of Positive Thinking in Business*, author Scott W. Ventrella lists these characteristics associated with positive thinkers:

- ✓ Optimism
- ✓ Enthusiasm
- ✓ Belief
- ✓ Integrity
- ✓ Courage
- ✓ Confidence
- ✓ Determination
- ✓ Patience
- ✓ Calmness
- ✓ Focus

Correlate these to the case study presented.

Handout 33.1
Case Study

Situation

John Foster is an employee in the finance department of XYZ company. His immediate supervisor is Dave Albright. A firm believer in continuous improvement, John has noticed certain changes that could be made to improve the company—changes that would require top-level approval to implement. One day, John decides to take the initiative and write up an improvement report to submit to the CEO of XYZ. Before submitting the report, though, John asks Dave to review it. Days later, John learns his report has been submitted to the CEO. The problem? Dave has put *his* name on the report instead of John's. To compound the difficulty of the situation, John hears the CEO is preparing to give a cash award for the report… to *Dave*.

Discussion

- Discuss similar situations that have happened to you or someone you know.

- Describe in detail three approaches that will protect the careers of all involved and will resolve this situation.

- Describe in detail three ways in which the situation could have been avoided.

- Describe changes/repercussions that could result from this situation.

Submitted by: Regina Robertson
                      Phone: (505) 301-2762
                      E-mail: bellwhistles@aol.com

Regina Robertson is a management and leadership director. She has been employed by the federal government for 24 years. She also owns and operates her own business and training media company, Bells and Whistles.

Reproduced from *50 Reproducible Activities for Promoting Ethics Within the Organization*, by Marlene Caroselli. HRD Press, 2015.

34. Ethical Management
Alphabet Soup-ervision

Approximately 25 minutes (more or less, depending on size of class)

OVERVIEW
Everyday acronyms are given new meaning in this exercise and then are related to ethical situations that managers may need to resolve.

PURPOSE
To encourage creative thinking regarding ethical decisions managers may face.

GROUP SIZE
Any size group, divided into subgroups of three or four.

ROOM ARRANGEMENT
If possible, table groups for three or four participants at each.

MATERIALS
- Handout 34.1, *"Acronymically Yours"*
- **Optional:** Bag of candy

PROCEDURE
1. Introduce the exercise by noting the assertion by author Michael Michalko that geniuses force relationships. And that today, you're going to ask them to force some relationships that will, ideally, lead to new approaches to old management problems.

2. Distribute Handout 34.1 and permit sufficient time for completion of it—at least 15 minutes.

3. Bring closure to the exercise by asking a spokesperson from each group to report on the work they've done, noting especially a new solution for a management problem encased in the new acronym meaning.

VARIATION
The practice of forcing relationships between things not usually connected will benefit those seeking to improve their verbal fluidity or ability to think on their feet. Provide any series of letters, such as F-I-K-D-E, and challenge teams to create as many full sentences as they can within five minutes. The only rules are that the sentences must contain a subject and a predicate, and once a word has been used, it *cannot* be used again in any of the other sentences. An example of

191

this combination would be "Fickle insurers kindle dedicated energies"—not a literary masterpiece, but a sentence nonetheless.

DISCUSSION
- What does your manager do to encourage novel thinking in those who report to him or her?

- What patterns among managerial problems have you noticed emerging in the years you have served as a manager or the years during which you have worked for a manager?

- What does it say to a staff when a manager tries out a novel approach?

QUOTATION
"The fool wonders, the wise man asks."

– Benjamin Disraeli

POINTS OF INTEREST
The other seven strategies* cited by Michalko are:

- ✓ Looking at problems in many different ways.
- ✓ Making thoughts visible.
- ✓ Demonstrating immense productivity.
- ✓ Making novel combinations.
- ✓ Thinking in opposite terms.
- ✓ Thinking metaphorically.
- ✓ Preparing for chance.

Ask participants to relate these to ethical dilemmas they have faced in the past.

*Reprinted with permission from "Thinking Like a Genius," by Michael Michalko, *Window on the Future*, http:/www.newhorizons.org.

Handout 34.1
Acronymically Yours

Directions

Step 1: These are common acronyms in the world of business. For each, replace the actual meaning with a group-created, work-related meaning. For example, RFQ—instead of "Request for Quotation," it could be replaced with "Reasons for Quitting."

Acronym	Current Meaning	New Meaning
WIIFM	What's In It For Me?	_____
NIMBY	Not In My Backyard	_____
FYI	For Your Information	_____
ASAP	As Soon As Possible	_____
PDQ	Pretty Darn Quick	_____
CC	Carbon Copy	_____
KISS	Keep It Simple, Silly	_____
BTW	By The Way	_____
GMTA	Great Minds Think Alike	_____

Step 2: Select any one of the new meanings and, as a group, discuss it in relation to these prompts.

1. Considering the new meaning, what direct, ethics-related experience have you (or others you know or know of) had with it? (For example, have you ever felt like quitting [RFQ] because of an unethical action taken by your manager? What prevented you from quitting? Or, do you regret quitting?)

2. How was the situation resolved or does it continue to this day?

3. If you could create the perfect circumstances surrounding this issue, what would you do that is not already being done?

35. Ethical Management
Manager–Management

Approximately 30 minutes

OVERVIEW
Nonmanipulative communication is the focal point of this exercise, which asks participants to consider the ethics of strategies involved in both upward and downward communicating. The reporting stage of the exercise fosters good listening and quick thinking.

PURPOSE
- To examine the communication process.
- To explore the ethical aspects of steps in that process.

GROUP SIZE
Any size group. Participants will first work alone and then in pairs.

ROOM ARRANGEMENT
No special seating required.

MATERIALS
- Equipment for displaying PowerPoint slides
- Slide 35.1, *"Upward Communication"*

PROCEDURE
1. Begin with a brief discussion of the three types of communication in the business world: "upward," to those in positions higher than one's own; "downward," to those serving in subordinate positions; and "lateral," to those on an organizational level similar to one's own. Ask how the tone of such communications will differ.

2. Ask participants to work in pairs. (**Note:** If there is one person "left over," he or she can form a triad with some pair.) Ask them to assume that one person in the partnership is the employee and the other person is his or her manager.

3. Ask the "subordinate" to list at least five key points in communicating upward and ask the "manager" to list at least five recommendations for communicating downward. Have everyone asterisk the one point on their lists they regard as most important.

4. Begin a round-robin of responses. Start with the "subordinates": have a "subordinate" stand and state his or her asterisked point. Call for immediate response: Do other class members think the recommendation is manipulative? Do they endorse it? Would they use it, et cetera. (**Note:** The response part of this exercise must move very quickly.) Then call on the second "subordinate" to give his or her most important point. Ask for input and then move on to the next. Continue until all the subordinates have had a chance to speak.

5. Continue the process by having each "manager" provide his or her most important point, followed by immediate and rapid feedback.

6. Display Slide 35.1, *"Upward Communication,"* based on an article by William Tracey, president of Human Resources Enterprises of Cape Cod, Inc., who asserts that the key to effective boss management is communication. He gives these suggestions for prudent response when someone is being attacked by a boss or is simply in disagreement with a boss. Ask participants to comment on the ethical nature of the recommendations. Are there any with which participants disagree?

7. Debrief the exercise with a summary based on the Discussion questions.

VARIATION
Many of the understanding gaps between managers and employees can be closed by asking each to list their views on a certain issue. For example, the employee might list what he or she thinks is needed in order for him or her to be promoted. That employee's manager would make the same list. Then, the employee and his or her manager would meet to compare their lists, discuss the differences, and perhaps prioritize steps on a career path.

DISCUSSION
*   Is manipulation, like sexual harassment, determined by the recipient of such behavior or by the person engaged in the behavior?
*   Under what conditions is manipulative behavior acceptable? (For example, parents often engage in such behavior with their children and vice versa. Is this acceptable? Why or why not?)
*   If you realize an attempt at manipulation is being made, does the attempt then seem less offensive? Why or why not?
*   What causes some people to be offended by such behavior and others to be not in the least affected by it?

QUOTATION
"Character is much easier kept than recovered."
– Thomas Paine

POINTS OF INTEREST

Peter Belanger, president of Outbound Resources, Inc., of Van Nuys, California, endorses the concept of "conceding before continuing." He recognizes that in the minds of many, conceding is synonymous with failure or a loss of power. Yet, in an insightful contrarian view, he suggests backing off from a communication exchange. Such a tactic, he asserts, melts resistance and begins a relationship established on trust.

These are some of the phrases with which he concedes:

- ✓ "I don't think I can be of any help to you at all today."
- ✓ "Why don't I leave you alone for a few months?"
- ✓ "Sounds like you're up to your eyeballs in training already."
- ✓ "Your plate is full. Let me check back with you around (date)..."

Slide 25.1

Upward Communication

- Never reply immediately.
- Ask for time to stop and think.
- Ask yourself what you want to happen.
- If time permits, rehearse your reply.
- Keep your voice soft.
- Ask the boss what he or she would like you to do.
- Listen to the response and repeat it.
- State what you want, but be willing to negotiate.
- Always let the boss have the last work.

35.1

36. Ethical Management
You Know There's a Child

Approximately 20 minutes

OVERVIEW
Participants are asked to take a long and hard look at the elements within their workplace that constitute ethical management. Although the exercise begins on a light-hearted note, it quickly becomes a strong-headed compilation of ideas managers can incorporate into their own managerial style. The exercise concludes with a panel discussion.

PURPOSE
To compile a list of ways to demonstrate ethical management is being practiced.

GROUP SIZE
The size should be big enough to accommodate a panel presentation with enough people in the audience to listen and interact with the panelists.

ROOM ARRANGEMENT
Seating flexible enough to accommodate small groups and then a panel arrangement in the front of the room with the other seats arranged audience-style.

MATERIALS
- Equipment for displaying PowerPoint slides
- Slide 36.1, *"You Know There's a Child in the House..."*

PROCEDURE
1. Begin by showing Slide 36.1. Ask for other examples that offer proof that a child or children live in a particular house.

2. Segue to the exercise by pointing out that ethical management—and unethical management as well—can be easily spotted by customers, subordinates, and senior managers alike.

3. Ask small groups to list, as specifically as possible, actions and words that demonstrate a moral climate and those that evince breaches of ethics.

4. Then advise the groups they'll be selecting a spokesperson to serve on a panel. The selection can be made in one of two ways: either the person who is most comfortable addressing a group can serve as spokesperson *or* the person who is *least* comfortable but who knows he or she needs to gain more experience.

5. Have the spokespersons come forward with their lists and form a panel, which you will moderate with these discussion questions, and others if you wish. Involve the audience as much as possible.

VARIATION
The same construct ("You know there's a _____ in the organization if/when....") may be used for Leadership, Coaching, Teambuilding, Supervision, and many other classes. The lists, once compiled, can be shared with future classes, can be published, and can be sent to participants' managers as an example of one of the instructional points made in the class.

DISCUSSION
*   Which is more powerful: truth or perception?

*   To what extent are ethics truthfully manifest in your organization?

*   To what extent does the perception of an ethical environment pervade the organization?

*   Does your manager consciously think about creating an ethical environment?

*   Does he or she think about creating the *appearance* of one?

*   What evidence do you have of either the reality or the perception of reality, as far as an ethical culture is concerned?

QUOTATION
"I shall adopt new views as fast as they shall appear to be true views."
        – Abraham Lincoln

POINTS OF INTEREST
A survey conducted by the Ethics Resource Centre in Washington, D.C., found that 60 percent of American companies have formal codes of ethics for doing business both domestically and abroad. Typically, these codes encompass the treatment of customers, suppliers, shareholders, employees, and the communities in which the firms are doing business.

Slide 36.1

"You know there's a child in the house if...

...you have to wash the soap before using it."

36.1

37. Ethical Management
Will the Real Ethical Manager Please Stand?

Approximately 25 minutes

OVERVIEW
This exercise attempts to close the gap between perception and reality by encouraging managers to assess themselves as they believe others see them and then to assess themselves as they see themselves.

PURPOSE
To develop awareness of the gap between perceptions of ethical behavior and the reality on which those perceptions are based.

GROUP SIZE
Any size group. Participants will first work alone and then in triads. (**Note:** This exercise works best with people who know each other well or participants who have worked together for most of the session. It's best not to use it early in the training day but rather after participants have had an opportunity to get to know one another.)

ROOM ARRANGEMENT
Seating that can accommodate the formation of three-person subgroups.

MATERIALS
Handout 37.1, *"Ethics Profile"* (**Note:** Each person should receive two copies: one to work on in class and the second to be taken back to the office, copied, and distributed to the manager's staff.)

PROCEDURE
1. Lead a brief discussion of the causes for discrepancies in the way we see ourselves and the way others see us.

2. Explain that you're going to distribute a self-assessment for the purpose of helping participants determine if a gap exists between their self-perception and the perception others may have of them.

3. Stress repeatedly that perceptions are not truth. If someone perceives managers in a more negative fashion than they perceive themselves, the other person is not necessarily right. The exercise is intended only to open dialogue, to explore why the difference might exist. It is not intended to label participants.

4. Encourage participants to substantiate their answers if they can with specific references that may have led to their perceptions. This substantiation should be done both as they fill out the assessment individually, and then after, as they discuss it in triads.

5. Distribute the assessment form, Handout 37.1, *"Ethics Profile,"* and allow time for participants to complete it.

6. Form triads and encourage sensitive and supportive analyses and differences of opinion.

7. Ask each triad to characterize the nature of their discussions: For example, were they conducted in a professional, sensitive, nonthreatening manner.

8. Debrief by asking one person in each triad to share his or her characterizations. Conclude with a strong recommendation that participants/managers use the form with their staff members and that they conduct subsequent discussions in the most professional manner possible.

VARIATION

Ideally, participants will take the assessment back to the workplace and make a copy for everyone whom they manage. To encourage honest responses, appoint one person to collect the completed (anonymous) surveys and to give them all at once to the manager. At a subsequent meeting (either one-on-one or with the staff as a whole), the manager—if he or she is brave enough—can stimulate dialogue regarding ways to improve.

DISCUSSION

- What causes some people to wear "blinders" when it comes to their own behavior?

- Think of a time in your work life when someone misjudged you. Did he or she ever come to know the real you? What barriers were created by that incident?

- How often do you think the average person does an assessment of the way he or she sees himself or herself and of the way others see him or her?

QUOTATION
"Underpromise, overdeliver."

– Joel Pliskin

POINTS OF INTEREST
Writing in *Executive Excellence*, Paul Evans, a professor of organizational behavior at INSEAD, maintains "your assets are your potential liabilities."

Your successes lead to a predictable self-confidence. But excessive self-confidence, especially for those in authority, can lead a "pendulum swing toward failure."

Handout 37.1
Ethics Profile

Directions

Actions, like most other things, are neutral in and of themselves. They can be executed, however, in an ethical or unethical manner; they can fall anywhere on the ethical continuum. Music, for example, is a neutral concept. When blasted 24/7, it can be torture for those in a prison camp. When performed harmoniously, it can provide an enchanted evening for hundreds of music lovers.

Look at the actions that you engage in as a manager. Then rate yourself on the ethical continuum by placing an "X" to show the manner in which you typically perform this action or the rationale behind your undertaking of this action. Consider genuine concern for others versus advancing your own cause or self-aggrandizing.

1.   **Socializing**

Shamefully Unethical ——————————————————————— *Extremely Ethical*

2.   **Volunteering**

Shamefully Unethical ——————————————————————— *Extremely Ethical*

3.   **Tolerating**

Shamefully Unethical ——————————————————————— *Extremely Ethical*

4.   **Promoting the Department/Member**

Shamefully Unethical ——————————————————————— *Extremely Ethical*

5.   **Seeking Perfection**

Shamefully Unethical ——————————————————————— *Extremely Ethical*

6.   **Showing Sensitivity**

Shamefully Unethical ——————————————————————— *Extremely Ethical*

Handout 37.1: *Ethics Profile* (concluded)

7. **Achieving Goals**

Shamefully Unethical ——————————————— *Extremely Ethical*

8. **Compromising**

Shamefully Unethical ——————————————— *Extremely Ethical*

9. **Persuading**

Shamefully Unethical ——————————————— *Extremely Ethical*

10. **Persisting**

Shamefully Unethical ——————————————— *Extremely Ethical*

Reproduced from *50 Reproducible Activities for Promoting Ethics Within the Organization,* by Marlene Caroselli. HRD Press, 2015.

38. Ethical Management
Codified Ethics

Approximately 40 minutes

OVERVIEW
For those who manage but have not yet managed to establish a code of ethics, this exercise first asks participants to read a monograph regarding standards and then to incorporate specific values into a set of principles by which employees can interact honestly and respectfully.

PURPOSE
To create a set of standards for use in the workplace.

GROUP SIZE
Any size group. Participants will first work alone and then in subgroups of three to five participants.

ROOM ARRANGEMENT
Flexible seating that allows the formation of subgroups.

MATERIALS
Handout 38.1, Monograph: *"Establishing a Code of Ethics"*

PROCEDURE
1. Introduce the activity by asking if anyone has a special ethical principle—such as, "Do unto others as you would have others do unto you"—that governs everyday behavior. Briefly discuss these and then explain that they'll be working today to prepare a set of such principles for the workplace.

2. Distribute the Handout 38.1, Monograph: *"Establishing a Code of Ethics."* Allow at least 10 minutes for participants to **read just the section titled "Integrity Gauges."** Encourage them to underline points they find interesting and to write questions/comments in the margins. Tell them if they finish, they should go to any other section of the monograph that interests them.

3. Ask them to review their underlinings/notes and to formulate a set of ethical principles, simply stated, to govern interactions in the workplace—without duplicating the questions asked in the monograph. After a few minutes, ask them to stop reading. Remind them that they weren't expected to read the entire monograph: "There is no way you could have finished reading the whole monograph, but it belongs to you. You can finish it at another time.

Right now, you probably have read enough and have made enough notes to form a small group to discuss the questions asked regarding integrity gauges."

4. Form subgroups of three or four and have participants work to discuss the questions that made up the integrity gauges. They will next formulate statements embodying an effective ethics code for the workplace. Their statements could be in the form of declarative or interrogative statements.

5. Ask a spokesperson from each subgroup to leave the room with the list of his or her group's synthesized principles. In a breakout room (or a corner of the classroom, if no other room is available), ask the subgroup representatives to synthesize their lists.

6. As they do so, facilitate a forum with the remaining participants, using the Discussion questions and Points of Interest as guideposts.

7. Bring closure to the exercise by having a spokesperson from the group composed of subgroup representatives report on their work.

VARIATION
Ask for a volunteer to obtain permission to have these principles printed and distributed throughout the organization.

Assign different subgroups different sections of the monograph so that subsequent reports can be made on the monograph as a whole.

DISCUSSION
- What principles that you acquired during childhood still guide you today?

- Do you think America has become a "kinder, gentler" nation since President Bush first hoped we could, more than a decade ago?

- In your opinion, what ethical guidelines govern your organization's treatment of employees, customers, and others directly or indirectly affected by the product or service you provide?

QUOTATION
"We are what we repeatedly do. Excellence, then, is not an act, but a habit."
                                                                    – Aristotle

POINTS OF INTEREST

Gerald Frisch, president of GFA, Inc., and managing director of the National Cost Reduction Institute, recommends policy-implementers first consider six areas before they attempt to establish a new policy, such as a code of ethics for everyone to follow:

- ✓ The Big Picture (Look at the overall communications process.)

- ✓ History (Look at the success rate of other implementations.)

- ✓ Memory (Ask employees what they thought about and what they did or didn't do when other, earlier implementations were put in place.)

- ✓ Conferences (Set up conferences with employees and review the reports and data used to arrive at certain decisions.)

- ✓ Dialogue (Have employees swap experiences regarding their understanding and acceptance of management directives.)

- ✓ Payoff (Determine the benefits to top management, employees, and the culture itself.)

Handout 38.1
Establishing a Code of Ethics

In this monograph, four-quadrant correlates are made between the worth of a given project and the need to manipulate others to accept it. Generally speaking, the higher the worth, the easier it is to involve others. The problems and solutions associated with influencing in various quadrants are explored as a means of understanding the gestalt or integrated structures within which influence occurs.

More specific information regarding the foreground and background of influence is found in the gauges by which integrity is assessed. If the team of influencer and influencees agrees on the need for a code of ethics and if they are willing to develop it, they will have a set of ground rules to govern present and future eventualities. A number of questions need to be considered in the shaping of this code.

As the influence team works together, they move through distinct stages. The influencer can expect initial resistance or balking. He overcomes this first barrier by talking about the project and its multiple benefits. He monitors the implementation of the project, looking for and patching cracks in the structural integrity as they occur. At some point, the influencer can walk away from the project, confident that others are so immersed in its worth that they will carry on without him. But the distancing is never total: the influencer maintains a loose but ongoing connection with those who are maintaining the project, even after he has moved on to new projects.

No matter what projects the influencer is engaged in, he will find value in the ROR-Shock Model, which improves on reality by reifying the ideal or making a concrete reality where only aspirations existed before. If such work is approached with an open mindset, benefits can be derived for more individuals than the two parties usually involved in seeking Win/Win outcomes. A liberated mindset can lead to Win/Win/Win results.

MANIPULATION

Low   High
Manipulation   Worth

■ ■ ■ ■ ■ ■   ■ ■ ■ ■ ■ ■

High   Low
Manipulation   Worth

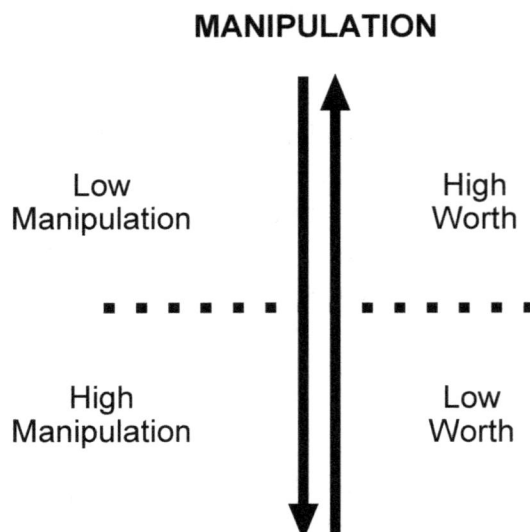

Manipulation is unhealthy, for influencer and influencee alike. As shown in the diagram above, the lines indicating manipulation and worth are parallel but diametric in value: the more manipulation you feel you have to use, the less worth your concept typically has (or the less creativity you have found to promote the concept).

Manipulative influencers are not typically truthful or open in their transactions; they do not tell the whole story; they move others toward ends that are less than honorable or toward results that have been fraudulently or unfairly earned. The word "manipulate" actually has honest origins—the Latin word, *manus*, meaning "hand." (Those who used their hands well or who could handle tools well were said to be manipulative. Even today, this meaning is the first given in most dictionaries for the word "manipulate.")

And of course there are some who learn to handle themselves, others, and situations so skillfully that their actions seem contrived. So polished are they in their presentations, so adept at understanding what motivates people, that they appear to go into automatic pilot in dealing with both expected and unexpected occurrences. After a while, their facility with words seems glib, their smoothness too slick, their sincerity suspect. In the extreme, there are those with an uncanny ability to "psych out" other people, to sense what they want to hear and then deliver it. But such individuals form the ranks of fortunetellers and psychic healers, not the realm in which influencers use integrity as their coin of commerce.

If manipulation seems an easy way out or a quick fix, it very well may be—but not for long. What you lose in reputation and stature will be far more costly than what you gain in expediency. Most people can be exploited once, but will then be distrustful for a long time after.

The overriding goal of influence is working with others to achieve a goal everyone has bought into. When you are the only one supporting the plan, despite repeated efforts, and find yourself using any means to reach the end, you may as well abandon the effort—*if* your intent was to influence with integrity. Influence may not *begin* with everyone in accord regarding the worth of the end product. However, during the process and by the end of the process, everyone participating has opted for involvement and has agreed to the mission and the work required to reach that mission.

Using horizontal arrows to represent these extremes, our diagram would look like this:

Low Involvement	⟶	Willing Participation
High Conflict	⟵	Low Conflict

If we were to use both sets of describers, the complete diagram would have four quadrants, which we'll label Q1, Q2, Q3, and Q4.

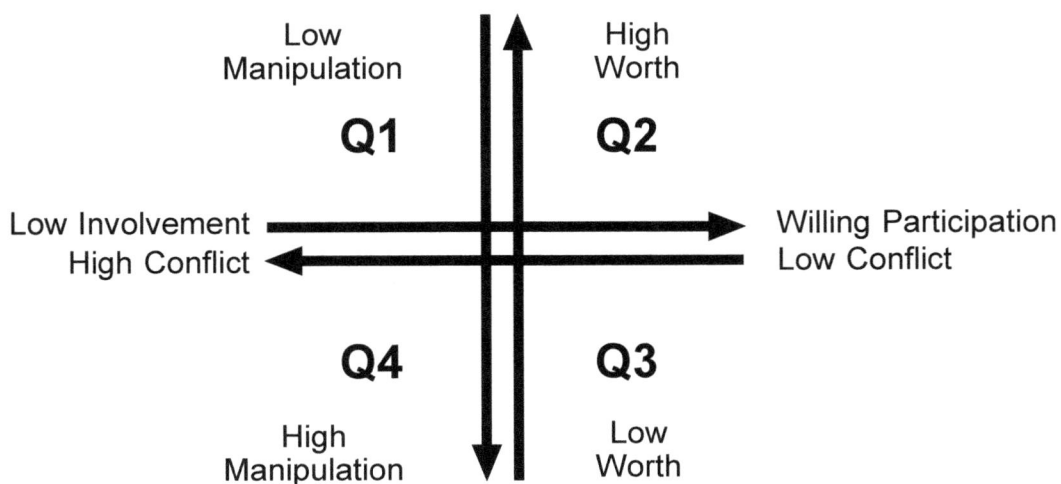

	Low Manipulation **Q1**	High Worth **Q2**	
Low Involvement High Conflict	⟷	⟷	Willing Participation Low Conflict
	High Manipulation **Q4**	Low Worth **Q3**	

Handout 38.1: *Establishing a Code of Ethics* (continued)

Quadrant Characteristics

Think about some person or group you have recently influenced. Then read the four descriptions that follow and determine which one best fits these influencing circumstances.

Q1: Low Manipulation/Low Involvement

People who are distinctly nonmanipulative may or may not be able influencers. If they are not, they fall into this first quadrant. They inspire little or low involvement on the part of those whom they wish to make part of their mission. Typically, they have intensive commitment to their plan but lack extensive power over others. To be sure, some plans can be executed by a committee of one (if you are trying to influence your supervisor to give you a raise, for example), but more often you will need the synergy of a team to accomplish extraordinary feats.

What's the problem? Basically, the problem is a lack of confidence—in yourself, perhaps in the project, perhaps in other people. It's hard to lead if you are fearful, hard to convince others if you lack enthusiasm or commitment. Confidence may be lagging for other reasons as well: it may be the project is right but the circumstances are wrong, or the mix of personalities is not right. Also, if circumstances are dictating mood—if colleagues, for example, are worried about downsizing—the best and best-intentioned influencers will find confidence or enthusiasm almost impossible to muster. If the timing is wrong, little else will be right.

What's the solution? First consider the possible abandonment of this project. It may be better to reserve your energies for one you feel more strongly about. If abandonment is not the answer, you may have to examine your delivery style. If possible, tape record yourself (at least by audio if not video equipment). Afterward, with as much detachment as you can garner, critique yourself. Would *you* be willing to do something with or for the person on this tape on the basis of the delivery you are now hearing or watching?

There is another possibility if you feel your influencing is of the Q1 variety. Do some "exit" interviews. After an overture that did not involve or excite your prospective influencees, call them one by one, or meet with them, and simply ask, *"What could I have done differently that might have made you more involved?"*

Handout 38.1: *Establishing a Code of Ethics* (continued)

Q2: High Worth/High Willing Participation

The very fact that your project can be described as having high worth may be the reason participation in it is so willingly given. Little outright influencing is needed after presenting your plan to your influencees, for your idea is probably speaking for itself. Typically, in high worth/high willing participation situations, the individuals involved have worked together before or know each other well or know you well. Consequently, trust and positive feelings run high.

What's the problem? There is a danger here, however. It's called groupthink. When the members of a group like each other and the leader, they are less contentious or questioning than they might otherwise be. The unspoken need to conform socially may in fact cause some decisions to be made before their time.

What's the solution? Ask one person (ideally, the most analytical thinker among you) to deliberately play the role of devil's advocate. He or she will purposely rain on the collective parade whenever it seems the group is being swept away by its own enthusiasm. This person will ask questions, cite data, get outside opinions— whatever is necessary to ensure final decisions have been subjected to the scrutiny they deserve.

Q3: Low Conflict/Low Worth

Properly channeled, conflict may be the best thing that can happen to your influence efforts. But it must be the kind of conflict that is characterized by debate rather than vitriolic observations. If there is low conflict, there is probably low interest. As a group moves from the opening stage of the project (at which they are assembling and getting to know one another) to the conflict stage, questions, challenges, and territoriality issues can and should emerge. Until agendas are uncovered and conflict resolved, the team will not be able to move to the productive stage (at which agreement is reached on operational concerns) and will not ever achieve the accomplishment stage (at which objectives are met). If there is little external conflict, there may be little worth associated with the project. People simply do not care enough to object to it.

What's the problem? There may be two problems associated with low conflict/low worth. The lack of conflict may not be a lack of interest at all. Rather, something else may be governing the reactions of those you have chosen to influence. For example, if your position is senior to theirs, they may not be speaking up for fear of jeopardizing their standing.

Handout 38.1: *Establishing a Code of Ethics* (continued)

What's the solution? One way to move the group to debate is to use Delphi deliberations, a group dynamics technique originated by the ancient Greeks. Simply ask those you wish to be involved in your project to anonymously record their thoughts about its worth, about their feelings at the moment, about what you have said so far, et cetera. Then ask them to fold their papers and pass them to you. One at a time, you can read the comments (paraphrasing as necessary) and open each to discussion, and to the conflict that is so healthy to progress.

If the majority continue to evince little faith in the project, you will either have to resell it, repackage it, reject it, or resurrect it later.

Q4: High Manipulation/High Conflict

By the time most of us are old enough to enter the workforce, we know when we are being conned and know we do not like it. Only the truly naive can be manipulated without some conflict erupting within them. It may be only a voice whispering inside their heads "This isn't right" or "This is too good to be true." But, almost always, there will be an indication that we are in danger of being duped. (Similarly, the manipulator knows when he or she is operating in a manipulative fashion.)

The conflict may take any one of several forms: self-doubt, discomfort, worry, stress, or fear. Or, it may be expressed in the form of verbal conflict with the manipulator. Suspicion leads some to resort to a more covert means of resolving the conflict within them, such as initiating a background check or using hidden cameras.

What's the problem? If your intuition/common sense/past experience/friends are telling you something is wrong, something probably is. The internal conflict you are experiencing is the best reason to investigate the situation further. Chances are, someone is withholding information you need before making up your mind to commit your time, savings, or heart to this individual.

What's the solution? Stall. Before committing yourself or your funds, ask for more time. Then confer with others to learn more about the potential manipulator and his or her history. Of course, some issues don't warrant such investments. In these cases, you can simply but firmly ask, "Is there something you're not telling me?" You could also tell the manipulator that you are not comfortable doing what he or she has asked of you and let that be the end of it.

Integrity Gauges

As we've noted, most people know when they are manipulative and most people know when they are being manipulated. Nonetheless, neither families, schools, nor businesses can operate on the assumption that individuals will recognize manipulation when they use it and when it is being used on them. It is much better to have a clearly articulated set of principles for the ethical conduct of family affairs, school practices, and business operations. Two questions precede the asking of questions that will lead to the formation of ethical guidelines: Can we agree that we need a code of ethics? If you and/or the group with whom you are interacting answer yes, then the next question is: Are we willing to develop that code?

In a sense, the macrocosmic code of ethics is like the microcosmic set of ground rules that governs team meetings. Based on integrity, honor, and respect, the code clearly stipulates what is proper and what will not be tolerated in various circumstances. For many, a gauge of sorts is useful. A number of these are available or can easily be created, to assist in the decision making that confronts us on a daily basis. For example, in 1932, businessperson Herbert J. Taylor developed a four-way test for evaluating our intended actions:

- ✓ Is it the truth?

- ✓ Is it fair to all concerned?

- ✓ Will it build goodwill and better friendships?

- ✓ Will it be beneficial to all concerned?

In keeping with such interrogative introspections, these are but a few of the additional questions that can be raised to form the framework within which integrity can drive influence.

- ✓ Could this harm us in any way?

- ✓ Could it harm others?

- ✓ Is it legal?

- ✓ Does it feel wrong?

- ✓ If the customer could see us doing this, would he or she be willing to pay for it?

- ✓ Would I still do this if news of it were broadcast in tomorrow's newspaper?

Handout 38.1: *Establishing a Code of Ethics* (continued)

- ✓ Would we be proud to do this with our families watching?

- ✓ Who will be the primary beneficiary of this action? The secondary beneficiary?

- ✓ Are there safety/union/OSHA issues we may have overlooked?

- ✓ What actions would constitute violations of ethical conduct?

- ✓ What are the consequences of violations?

- ✓ In what ways might we be, even unknowingly, pressuring others to act unethically?

- ✓ How do we maintain quality when we have to do more with less?

- ✓ In different circumstances (transculturally, for example), how might our tolerance limits change?

- ✓ Should we consider creating hot lines or an ombudsman position?

- ✓ How and how often should the code be disseminated?

- ✓ What complex or confusing situations might make our ethical guidelines murky in the eyes of some?

- ✓ What could cause confidence to be shattered?

- ✓ Does this action advance our mission?

- ✓ Is this action in keeping with our values?

- ✓ Would we be proud to say afterward that we were a part of this action?

- ✓ What assurances could we give regarding possible outcomes?

- ✓ Could we be rewarding unethical behavior in any way?

- ✓ What could we point to in the past that shows we have an ethical track record?

- ✓ What ethical messages are we sending or failing to send to others?

- ✓ Do people know what to do or to whom to turn if they have concerns about ethical conduct?

- ✓ If we could develop an Intranet message regarding integrity, what would it say?

The Influence Continuum

Assume that you have asked and satisfactorily answered these and other questions about the influence you wish to exert on others. You are convinced that what you want them to do (buy your product, give you a raise, join your team, support your candidacy, et cetera) is a worthwhile pursuit. Now it's time to influence them. You can expect to move through five basic stages: Balk, Talk, Caulk, Walk, and Stalk. For the sake of illustrative convenience, let's assume you are a workplace leader, interested in influencing others to apply more creativity to their problem-solving and decision-making situations.

You agree with Ken Blanchard that the key to leadership is influence not authority. Because you are in a peer rather than superior position, you feel an influence strategy is the only one that will work. Imagine this is your first meeting to explain what you hope others will do.

Balk

You can expect resistance, perhaps even naked rebellion, because your proposal involves change. Most people feel little need to give up a current practice and adopt one that seems to offer little improvement over their existing practice. Be prepared for questions (especially "What's in it for me?"), for challenges ("I'm doing just fine the way I am" or "This is just another management attempt to get us to work harder without paying us more"), and for surface agreement that will probably not go deeper without subsequent intervention on your part ("It sounds good. I'll give it a try" or "It sounds good, but let me think it over").

Recommendations for Influencing Others During the "Balk" Stage (at which point they don't know much about your proposal and probably don't care)

1. Lay some groundwork, even if you are not able to spell out many details in advance. Set a climate of expectation in anticipation of the actual unveiling of the proposal.

2. Anticipate resistance and be ready for it; rehearse your responses ahead of the actual meeting.

3. Cite precedents whenever you can. Facts, figures, and benchmarking data from others in comparable circumstances will go a long way toward persuading your influencees of the validity of your idea.

4. Make a dramatic show or powerful presentation, if appropriate. For example, let's say you had trained three of your colleagues from another department to use the very problem-solving technique you want to share with this team. Bring the others to the meeting and ask one of the team members to throw out a problem germane to the workplace. Give everyone, yourself and the three other people as well, 5 minutes to write anonymous solutions.

    Collect the solutions, read them, have the team select the most feasible option, and then ask who wrote it. Ideally, it will be you or one of those trained in your technique. (If not, you can overcome your embarrassment with a light-hearted remark prepared for just this eventuality: *"Charlie must have secretly read my notes and used the technique without telling us he was going to."*)

Talk

Before you outline your remarks, give serious consideration to this question: What influences me to pay attention? What factors are compelling enough for me to try something I'm not eager to try? What or who persuades me and how? Think through these questions, perhaps even inviting input from others. Then use every effective technique you have (and have analyzed) as you work to persuade others ethically.

To illustrate, seasoned influencers often begin winning over their audience by acknowledging the emotions others may associate with the prospect being presented. One fun way to explore people's reluctance to change involves only an inexpensive purchase on your part. Buy a quart of buttermilk, keep it chilled. Minutes before you start your presentation, place it on the table with cookies and napkins. Tell people to help themselves and then occupy yourself with some papers. Meanwhile, an observer you've planted at the table will note who is willing to try something new and what reasons others give for declining to do so.

Use the observer's comments as a prelude to your remarks, explaining that you fully understand many people prefer to continue doing things the way they've always done them. Next, lead them to the realization that when nothing is ventured, nothing is gained.

Recommendations for Influencing Others
During the "Talk" Stage
(at which point others don't know but
are probably willing to listen)

1. Use visuals to supplement your message. These should constitute not more than half of your presentation. Don't overdo the dependence on numbers, however. They cannot replace the passionate proposal and the rationale for its execution. (Ideally, your message will be trimodally delivered: your voice, your verbiage, and your visuals will all be optimized.)

2. Draw a picture with your words. Whether you are using metaphors or simply verbalized pictures, help your prospective followers latch onto the possibilities you envision. A set of architectural blueprints *and* a full-scale, full-color drawing of what the completed project will look like depict the same possibility. Most of us, however, prefer looking at the artistic rather than the technical representation. And so it is with a verbal picture. Especially when you are hoping to inspire or motivate, as opposed to giving a technical briefing, you need to appeal to the head and the imagination and the emotions of your audience.

3. Acknowledge the downside—before others can. There is risk in every venture. By covering up or failing to mention the drawbacks or setbacks that might ensue, you are not only being dishonest but you are leaving yourself open to attack. Presented properly, the negatives may even add to the allure of your proposal by allowing you to cite the need for courage, for example, or the need for people with an adventurous spirit.

4. Make the talk bidirectional. The idea being shaped should be bounced back and forth several times, like a verbal ping-pong on the table of possibilities. Arousing interest means creating collective buy-in, and buy-in means welcoming feedback.

5. First ensure and then assure that the idea you are proposing is both doable and worth doing. Don't worry about aiming slightly higher than existing comfort levels—it's the only way to raise the bar of excellence and keep others aiming high as well.

Handout 38.1: *Establishing a Code of Ethics* (continued)

Caulk

Some people are organizational caulkers; they know how to keep the corporate ship watertight by filling seams or cracks with a soft-at-first substance that, when it hardens, is difficult to crack. Effective influencers are caulkers, in a sense. First, they scrutinize a given entity, such as the plan they hope to effect, and look for weak spots. Then, once the plan or program has been launched, they constantly assess its implementation—solving problems, obtaining further resources, and shoring up a weakening commitment in order to keep the plan afloat.

Recommendations for Influencing Others During the "Caulk" Stage (at which point others are working to cement ideas into an overall framework)

1. Agree on uniform measurements. Because we have an infinite capacity for misunderstanding one another, it's especially important for the influencer to establish clear and measurable gauges of success. Words alone cannot be counted on. For example, two different pronunciations of the word "bad" in this sentence—"It's not a bad idea"—would lead to either of two interpretations: "But it's really not a good idea" or "That idea actually has great potential." The quantitative measures, although they need not be used exclusively, are the ones that will tell us where and if caulking is needed.

2. When setbacks occur, remind others of past accomplishments. Sometimes the future seems too far away, the goal less distinct than it once was, the importance of the plan less pressing. The effective influencer expects the valleys in the topography of implementation. He restores flagging spirits by patching up the cracks that may occur along the way.

   Jack Kahn, for example, CEO of Manco, Inc., a manufacturer of duct tape, spurs his sales staff to ever-greater achievement by making promises ("A hairy challenge," *Incentive*, December 1997, page 12). He once promised that if sales quotas were met, he would shave off all his hair. Altered pictures of the nonhirsute executive were plastered throughout the workplace. A new record was set in sales, and as promised, the staff was allowed to shave the head of their chief executive.

3. Don't let defensiveness plug your ears. You won't be able to caulk if you don't know where the potential leaks may spring up. And you won't know where the leaks are if you refuse to listen to criticism. If you doubt the importance of caulking leaks, figurative or literal, let the following news story

convince you. As reported in *USA Today*, if repairs had been made in Chicago when leaks in the city's infrastructure were first noted, the cost would have been about $10,000. However, the caulking was not done, and as a result, 250 million gallons of water from the Chicago River spilled into underground pipes and then into the city, causing a loss of $1.5 billion attributable to repairs, lost revenue, and property damage.

4. Use the Five-Why technique for getting at root causes. This method of probing has you continuing to ask "Why?" until the real causes of problems are uncovered and not the superficial reasons.

Walk

There comes a point at which the leader's thrust recedes and the plan proceeds on the strength of its own momentum. In a sense, he or she has conceived of an idea, nurtured it through the long period of gestation, helped it get born and continue to grow. Then, as parents inevitably must do with their children, the influencer and influencees part ways. The leader usually moves on to another influence project, secure in the knowledge that his or her brainchild can now function on its own.

In terms of the change model espoused by Kurt Lewin (Thaw out, Introduce change, Re-freeze), the idea and its correlative change have been implemented. What remains now is the solidification of the plan. In this stage, the idea has been reified, it has become standard operating procedure, it has been made a familiar and permanent landmark in the organizational terrain.

**Recommendations for Influencing Others
During the "Walk" Stage
(at which point the influencer can walk away;
confident the vision is seen and supported by others)**

1. As the project draws to a close, think of appropriate ways to recognize those who have joined forces with you. One of the most remembered gestures is a formal letter of commendation, with a copy to the supervisor of those who participated in the project.

2. Bring closure to the collective undertaking by way of a ceremony or celebration of sorts. Not only does hard work on a special project deserve public and lavish praise, but such rituals also bespeak the natural ending of one cycle and the beginning of another. People often remember the closing ceremonies with as much intensity as they remember the many months preceding the project's conclusion.

Handout 38.1: *Establishing a Code of Ethics* (continued)

3. Encourage networking among those who have been part of the project. Frequently, all people need is a nudge in the right direction. While you, as the original influencer, need to keep in touch with them, they need to keep in touch with each other as well. Some teams find the initial success so heady an experience that they decide to undertake a second project. Other teams disband after the initial success, but network to keep alive memories of the past and hopes for the future.

4. Keep in mind those who have assisted you in the execution of a new idea as future projects arise. These may be projects of your own or plans being formulated by others. In the latter case, referrals of your recent influencees to influencers on future projects will be appreciated at both levels.

Stalk

Although this word has current negative associations, we use it in the sense of unexpectedly popping in on those who are carrying on with the project you have walked away from.

Recommendations for Influencing Others During the "Stalk" Stage (during which the influencer catches others doing the right things right)

1. Periodic progress reports will assure you as the influencer that the plan is being executed as you had hoped and that both it and the people putting it into action are able to act independently. You may have walked away from the project by the time this last stage is reached, but you have not walked out of their lives. Establish some means, formal or informal, of staying in touch with those who have worked with you to make your plan a reality.

   Your stalking need not take much time or trouble. The contacts can be made on a social level (an annual reunion) or on a communication level (a bi-annual newsletter with updates). But continue to show your interest in the new process or procedure that you have successfully influenced others to undertake.

2. When you make your phone calls or pop in on others, take the knowledge you're acquiring one step further. After you've witnessed the right things being done right, for example, suggest the organizational newspaper publish a feature article. Or, suggest that a new employee seek advice from those who served on the initial team.

Handout 38.1: *Establishing a Code of Ethics* (continued)

3. Discuss ways of continuously improving on the progress that's been made. Keep a record of the team's suggestions or a log of lessons learned, now that the plan is fully operational. Share these insights with those who may be starting a similar project of their own.

Graphically, the continuum depicting the steps you go through as you influence others to follow your ethical lead would look like this.

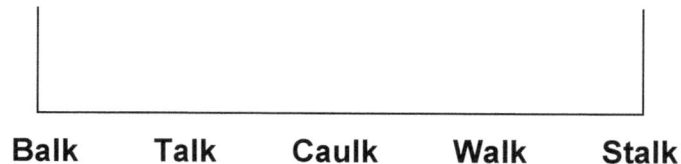

Balk   Talk   Caulk   Walk   Stalk

As influencees become more and more committed to the project put forth by the influencer, the effort you have to expend on influencing decreases, as shown in a second continuum line:

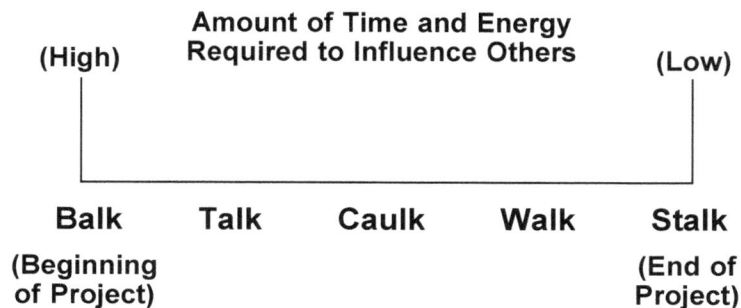

Amount of Time and Energy
Required to Influence Others

(High)   (Low)

Balk   Talk   Caulk   Walk   Stalk

(Beginning   **(End of**
of Project)   **Project)**

The five stages were explored within the context of a team situation, when the leader influences others, according to author Vance Packard's definition of leadership: "the art of getting others to want to do something that you are convinced should be done." The stages could apply, though, to a one-on-one scenario as readily as they do to a team setting. In the final stage, however, you would alter your approach somewhat.

To illustrate, if your purpose had been to influence your supervisor to give you a raise, you might have encountered initial resistance or balking. You next would have talked through and talked out the reason for the resistance, and ideally would have been successful in persuading him or her that you deserved a raise. Next, you would work throughout the appraisal year to make steady improvements in the quality of your work, caulking whatever deficiencies you found in your own performance.

Handout 38.1: *Establishing a Code of Ethics* (continued)

When your supervisor realizes you deserve not only the raise he or she gave you but future raises as well, then you can relax your influence efforts and in a sense walk away from the need to be convincing. However, you would never walk completely away; as you find yourself succeeding with one thing or another during the year, you would bring these efforts to the attention of your supervisor—in the most professional way possible.

Reality, Openness, Reification:
The ROR-Shock Model

Those who engage in ethical management take current reality and convert it to a new and improved reality, using openness as their medium. This is a process of reifying or creating something that didn't exist before. Essentially, it asks you to look at present realities; to remain open to the often-hidden opportunities that lie within the present; and then to reify or create a new reality.

Engaging in the process demands numerous skills, some of which you may not even realize you possess. That is why we call the model the ROR-Shock Model: you may be pleasantly surprised, if not sometimes shocked, to learn just how much potential you really have for effecting improvements on current practices.

Let's begin with a current **reality**. Think of some situation you are now facing—at home, at work, in a relationship, etc. The situation should be one that could be made better with proper influence on your part. Briefly describe that situation here.

_____

_____

_____

_____

_____

Next, let's gauge your **openness** for taking risks, for trying something new as you plan a strategy for reification, for making the future better than the present. Remember that selling a particular service, product, or proposal to others depends on your understanding of the current reality and your ability to remain mentally flexible or open to new ideas. Not until you have achieved these mental states can you create the new reality. It's often true that "if you build it, they will come," but if you don't hear or see the possibilities calling to you, you will never be able to turn them into realities.

Tips for Remaining Open to Possibilities
1. When key events, positive or negative, occur in your life, try to regard them as learning opportunities. Step back and depersonalize the situations, if you can. Regard them as gifts, even the worst of them, gifts that will strengthen you and maximize strengths you did not know you had.

Handout 38.1: *Establishing a Code of Ethics* (continued)

2. Develop the comfort you feel in various situations and various cultures. If you allow discomfort to overtake you, you cannot open yourself to the treasures embedded in experiences.

3. Work to form new partnerships, new relationships, new alliances. As they say about insanity, "Only a madman would do the same thing over and over and expect to have different results." To create new realities, you need new thoughts. That's impossible if you aren't having new experiences and if you aren't meeting new people.

4. Deliberately mix concepts, ideas, and possibilities that do not seem to go together at all. Ask yourself, for example, what would happen if you combined this with that, or if you changed this thing, or if you eliminated that?

5. Widen the camera angle from which you are viewing the world. Think about things that are happening in the outside world and the impact they might have upon what you are trying to do. Step away from the "brilliance of transient events," as Prussian military strategist Karl von Clausewitz described them, and think about long-range or short-range consequences that may result from them.

6. Alter the approach you typically use to solve problems and make decisions. With unprecedented situations, don't always gravitate to your old patterns. Make connections, if you can, between variables and people you would not typically consider.

Finally, having defined reality and having determined you are receptive to new possibilities, refer back to the reality you described on page 198. Think about the outcome you would like to see evolve from this situation. In other words, if you could be supremely effective in using your influence, how would this situation wind up? What would be the ideal outcome? What would lead to **reification**?

_____

_____

_____

_____

_____

_____

Discuss with others the steps needed to make this happen.

The Win3 Test

Win/Win Outcomes

You are no doubt familiar with the phrase "win/win" outcomes. It has long been used by upstanding and outstanding influencers to describe agreements that are satisfactory to both parties. When you as influencer, or others as influencees, operate from selfish stances or when compromise cannot be achieved, win/lose or even lose/lose results ensue.

Among the many techniques evinced by those who achieve ethical win/win results in business, the following are included:

- *Confident bargaining.* If you are fearful or uncertain about the benefits to be derived, you will exude hesitation, perhaps without even realizing you are doing so. Such revealing self-doubt may make others feel they can take unfair advantage of you. It will help if you start your influence sessions with a statement regarding your belief that the ultimate decisions can be satisfactory to all concerned.

- *Equitable exchanges.* If you are willing to do "x" now, ensure that others will do "y" tomorrow. An honest, reciprocal balance, established early on, sets the tone for the entire meeting. It may be as small an issue as the meeting room: "Fine. We can meet in your office today, but for the next meeting, let's meet in mine."

- *Astute understanding.* If you can develop a feel for the won't-budge, may-budge, will-budge positions others hold, you can streamline the process of influencing others to accept your own won't-budge, may-budge, and will-budge viewpoints. Even with the won't-budge issues, though, compromise is sometimes possible.

- *Temporal awareness.* They call it a cooling-off period when labor relations have become heated. We call it an awareness of how and when to use time. The best influencers understand when to be patient, when to suspend discussions, when to push for decisions, and when to let time intervene. Sometimes a caucus is called for or a time-out period. Silence itself often serves to promote reflection and ultimate resolution.

Handout 38.1: *Establishing a Code of Ethics* (continued)

Win3 Outcomes

We propose broadening the traditional definition of successful influence; that is, instead of outcomes acceptable to both parties, we encourage consideration of a third party (sometimes an abstract noun) that will benefit from influence exerted by those operating with integrity and those who respond to such influence. For example, you are applying for a job and have followed all the experts' advice on how to land it. You are properly groomed, you've done your homework about the company, your resume is polished, and you have rehearsed the questions you may be asked. If you are successful in your influence, you will be hired. And, of course, you will have a "win" outcome.

Assuming you have influenced with integrity, the other party will have a "win" outcome as well: your employer will have found the best person for the job. This simple example demonstrates the basic premise of influencing or even negotiating with integrity—that results prove beneficial to both the influencer and the influencee.

Now, though, we are asking that a third "win" be considered. Stretch your thinking. Who else or what else might benefit if in fact you are hired for this job? Keeping this third beneficiary in mind may even enhance your chances of getting the job. By identifying the third winner, you may be able to articulate a related goal.

Here's what we mean. Let's say you are eager to be hired because you have some ideas that, if implemented, will improve work processes. Yes, you want a job but you also want a chance to implement the things you have been thinking about. And yes, the employer will benefit.

But the Win3 thinker asks her- or himself if there is another entity that might profit. Assume you got the job. (You won.) Further assume your employer, after a three-month period, has already commended you for the improvements you have made. (He or she won, too.) Is there a way that your success might benefit others? Who could the third winner be? If you think along internal lines, you might offer to be an SME (subject matter expert) and share your knowledge with other employees working on similar processes.

Or, you could write an article for a trade journal. In this case, the third winner would be the reader, reaping the benefits of your improvements. (Actually, your employer would be a double winner, by way of the positive publicity that would accrue to the organization as your name and company are listed in the author blurb at the end of the article.)

Handout 38.1: *Establishing a Code of Ethics* (concluded)

Briefly outline three upcoming influence situations, three occasions when you will attempt to influence others to do something you truly believe should be done. Beneath each description, list the three win-beneficiaries and tell what they will win or how they will benefit.

Situation #1: _____

_____

_____

Winner A: _____ , because _____

Winner B: _____ , because _____

Winner C: _____ , because _____

Situation #2: _____

_____

_____

Winner A: _____ , because _____

Winner B: _____ , because _____

Winner C: _____ , because _____

Situation #3: _____

_____

_____

Winner A: _____ , because _____

Winner B: _____ , because _____

Winner C: _____ , because _____

Reproduced from *50 Reproducible Activities for Promoting Ethics Within the Organization*, by Marlene Caroselli. HRD Press, 2015.

39. Ethical Management
Stand Up for Standards

Approximately 60 minutes

OVERVIEW
This exercise enables leaders to explore their own ethical standards on a particular issue and to compare them to those of their colleagues. (They may subsequently decide to adjust their own standards on the basis of this comparison.)

PURPOSE
- To develop awareness of ethical standards—one's own as well as those of colleagues.
- To engage participants in the learning process known as peer learning.

GROUP SIZE
Any size group, divided into subgroups of four or five.

ROOM ARRANGEMENT
Ideally, table groups to accommodate four or five participants.

MATERIALS
- Flipchart and marking pens
- Handout 39.1, *"Assignment"*

PROCEDURE
1. Introduce the purpose and method of the exercise. Briefly discuss the meaning of Emerson's quotation, *"A foolish consistency is the hobgoblin of little minds."* Encourage participants to remain open to ideas that may conflict with their own.

2. Ask the group for suggestions on ethical issues that they feel unsure of and list these. If no suggestions are forthcoming, write up your own list. Suggestions follow.

   ✓ Hiring based on "who you know" rather than "what you know"

   ✓ Using paid time for private phone calls, Internet, e-mails, etc.

   ✓ Putting pressure on employees to work overtime, weekends, etc., to meet client workload

   ✓ Dressing up and dressing down on certain days

✓ Permitting "different strokes for different folks" or treating everyone the same

✓ Wining and dining clients: What's acceptable? What's not? Why not?

✓ Bending the rules for special circumstances: death in the family, prolonged illness, et cetera.

✓ Taking responsibility for employee welfare

✓ Facilitating employee career development (How far should this extend outside the current company career path?)

✓ Communicating honestly: To what extent are "white lies" or "sins of omission" acceptable? Toward employees? Toward clients?

3. Ask participants to vote on the issue (or issues, depending on the time allowed) that interest them most.

4. Next, form discussion subgroups based on their selections.

5. Give each group Handout 39.1, *"Assignment,"* and sufficient time to complete it—at least 30 minutes.

6. Bring the subgroups back together and let each in turn present their findings.

7. Highlight the differences in the standards of different individuals.

8. Lead a discussion regarding the causes of the differences. Determine, if possible, if the differences are acceptable in the organizational culture/climate.

9. Ask participants to share the extent to which the exercise influenced them.

10. Bring closure by asking each person to tell if his or her standards were altered at all after listening to colleagues' viewpoints. (If the group is large, allow time for subgroup discussion and then ask a spokesperson from each subgroup to present a synopsis.)

VARIATION
Ask everyone to think about a workplace issue with strong ethical overtones and to write their position regarding this issue on a scrap of paper. Call on five people (assuming a class size of 25) to stand and state their positions. Then ask the remaining participants to join one of the five groups that each of the five volunteers will lead. Participants should make their selection on the basis of their own feelings (of agreement or disagreement) regarding the positions taken by the five volunteers.

Allow the subgroups time to explore one another's viewpoint but also to achieve consensus, if they can, on a corporate position that should be taken regarding this particular issue.

DISCUSSION

- To what extent does the organization have the right to regulate personal freedom issues, such as groups of employees speaking in their native (non-English) tongue?

- Could it be dangerous to open certain topics to discussion? If so, how? Which topics?

- What current events may have/should have influenced your own organization's ethics policy?

QUOTATION

"Questions focus our thinking. Ask empowering questions like 'What's good about this?' 'What's not perfect about it yet?' 'What am I going to do next time?' 'How can I do this and have fun doing it?'"

– Charles Connolly

POINTS OF INTEREST

The sample issue of *Positive Leadership* provides an ethical checklist. These questions will help in the formation of both individual and organizational ethics policies.

- ✓ Is it legal?
- ✓ Is it fair and balanced?
- ✓ How will I feel when it's done?

Submitted by: Mike Morrell, Senior Consultant, Organizational and Staff Development
AtosOriginCOPM
Postbox 218
5600 MD Eindhoven
The Netherlands
Telephone: +31(0)6 – 53 17 50 71
E-mail: mikemorrell@atosorigin.com

Mike enjoys the process of discovering what it means to be a human being. He sees organizations and organizational development as the product of—and the current environment for—the further development of and interplay between individuals. He facilitates both organizational and individual staff development in the roles of trainer, coach, consultant, and change manager.

Handout 39.1
Assignment

a. Clarify what the issue is, how important it is, and give a few examples of work situations in which it is relevant.

b. Describe what your own ethical stance is with respect to this issue and compare this with any formal policy that you are aware of.

c. Describe how you adhere to your own ethical standards for this issue.

d. Describe what influence you have over others and how you use this.

e. Note the differences among the members of the subgroup on points (a) to (d).

f. Present your results at the plenary session.

Reproduced from *50 Reproducible Activities for Promoting Ethics Within the Organization*, by Marlene Caroselli. HRD Press, 2015.

40. Ethical Management
Perform as a Norm

45 to 60 minutes

OVERVIEW
Designed to boost performance levels, this exercise encourages participants to consider simple/workable/nonmanipulative ways to remove performance blocks and to develop employees' full potential.

PURPOSE
- To acquaint participants with positive tools for narrowing the gap between task demands and earmarked resources.
- To effect realization that fear is a negative and sometimes unethical way to motivate employees.

GROUP SIZE
Any size group, to be divided into subgroups of four or five.

ROOM ARRANGEMENT
If possible, table groups for four or five participants.

MATERIALS
- Flipchart and marking pens
- Equipment for displaying PowerPoint slides
- Slide 40.1, *"The Walk"*
- Slide 40.2, *"The Jump"*
- Slide 40.3, *"The Leap"*
- Slide 40.4, *"The Motivation"*

PROCEDURE
1. Begin by narrating the story of Tenali Rama and the Royal Banquet, as follows:

   Krishna Deva Raya, famous king of Vijaynagar (a powerful south Indian Empire of the 15th century), devised a test of his courtiers' resourcefulness. He invited them all to a grand banquet at the palace. Raya received the guests himself on the appointed day, and before leading them in to the banquet hall—all readied with rows of ornate chairs and silver plates and goblets—he laid down a seemingly small condition. The guests were to partake of the feast without flexing their elbows! The puzzled guests thought this a cruel joke and were about to turn away, clearly crestfallen, when the ever-resourceful Tenali Rama (the chief courtier and the king's confidant) came up with a workable solution that enabled them all to enjoy the banquet.

2. Ask the group to discuss a possible solution to the problem. Record their responses on a flipchart.

3. Share the solution: If each guest fed the guest to his left, none would have to bend their elbows. Discuss the answers from the perspective of practicality.

4. Emphasize the point that Tenali Rama succeeded by adapting to the awkward condition imposed by the king.

5. Conclude by pointing out that a shortfall between allocated resources and task demands is best bridged by adaptation, i.e., matching changes in operational conditions with suitable modifications in operational methods.

    Use these classic examples:

    -   Napoleon Bonaparte, when asked how he responded to unfavorable circumstances, replied, *"Unfavorable circumstances? Why, I always make my own circumstances and I never make them unfavorable."* To be sure, he kept his adversaries at bay by making suitable and necessary changes in his own strategies. He provides an excellent example of adapting to changing task demands.

    -   In World War II, bomber pilots learned to neutralize the newly developed RADAR tracking system, just by going out of range and flying at treetop level. They used their ingenuity to adapt to this potential threat of detection.

VARIATION
Draw parallels to occurrences the author experienced.

Once, sitting in his parked car on the roadside adjacent to an irrigation ditch, he saw a youngster and an old man (perhaps the grandfather) walking along the ditch on the far side of the road. (Display Slide 40.1 at this point.) At a narrow point of the ditch, the boy jumped across and waited for the old man to do likewise. (Show Slide 40.2 at this point.) But the old man stayed on his side and pointed to the stone slab across the ditch, a little way off. The old man said he thought it would be safer to use the slab than to jump over. After a couple of steps, however, the old man hitched up his dhothi (loincloth) and took a flying leap over the ditch. (Display Slide 40.3.)

Ask the group to discuss why the old man suddenly changed his mind. Have the groups note their answers in a few words on slips of paper. You can read these aloud and then lead a group discussion that compares their answers to this one (illustrated by showing Slide 40.4).

Answer: The physical capacity for leaping lay dormant in the old man, hidden under the imagined infirmities of old age. It only came alive when the motivation was provided by the rushing bull. The magic of motivation is that it unlocks dormant potential. All feats of mankind over the ages have been primed by motivation—whether those feats are accomplished by a single individual or by an entire team.

The group that came up with the correct answer is to be applauded.

Use this anecdote and a question or two to drive home the points emphasized, especially the fact that intractable managers are poor managers. During the author's seminar at the Air Force Technical College, Bangalore, a squadron leader (a maintenance officer) asked for suggestions on managing his civilian conservancy staff—most of whom were chronic absentees, latecomers, or those with alcohol problems. Questioning revealed that not a single person was guilty of all three problems. What was the remedy to be implemented? Let the groups discuss possibilities.

The author's suggestion was to take the absence of any of these vices as a virtue and allocate duties where the so-called virtues would be of maximum advantage. For example, the timely arrivals could be given early morning chores, nonabsentees could be given everyday cleaning jobs, and nondrinkers could do window cleaning, and so forth.

After several months, the officer called the author and confirmed that the remedy worked and he no longer had any problems. The moral of this true story: Your HRD policy will work only if you are humane.

DISCUSSION
- What's the best way for a manager to motivate his or her staff? Acknowledge that you cannot keep a mad bull in the office to chase people and thus provide motivation. Admit as well that it's human nature to do one's best for those one likes best and appreciates most. But, the best managers vow to treat everyone fairly. Respect for individuals, coupled with genuine concern for their problems and honest efforts to solve them, are the ingredients of a successful staff-motivation policy.

- Point out that a true leader will strive to keep himself/herself on an equal footing with subordinates as much as possible through practices such as: greeting them by name; making solicitous inquiries about their health, their families, their outside interests; and displaying ethical behavior at all times, thus setting the tone for others to follow. Such efforts typically yield results well beyond expectations.

QUOTATION

"The first problem for all of us, men and women, is not to learn, but to unlearn."
– Gloria Steinem

POINTS OF INTEREST

The story of the Yuks illustrates the need for caution when unleashing positive and powerful forces within the workplace. (It *is* possible to have too much of a good thing.) Sugar cane beetles were destroying the crops in Australia until scientists introduced a unique toad, nicknamed the "Yuk." Balance in the ecosystem was to have been achieved when the yuks destroyed the beetles and allowed the vegetation to thrive. Instead, the yuks thrived. They had no natural enemies and in time became more of a threat to the environment than the original beetles were.

The phenomenon has since come to be called the "yuk effect" and pertains to the downside of positive change. While it's admirable, as a rule, to encourage empowerment among employees, a workforce that is too empowered can assume authority that isn't rightfully theirs.

Submitted by: M. Vasudevam
                  No. 10, 8th Main
                  Sharada Colony
                  Basaweswaranagar
                  Bangalore 560 079 India
                  Phone: +91 (80) 348 5833
                  E-mail: mvasudevan_blr@hotmail.com

M. Vasudevan, Indian Institute of Science, Bangalore. Mr. Vasudevan has been a votary of maximizing efficiency in all spheres of human endeavor, with the aim of improving the welfare of humanity. He is a freelance writer and speaker on practical ways to boost productivity and has been the recipient of the State Government Award in 1991 and the National Award in 1984.

Slide 40.1

Slide 40.2

Slide 40.3

Slide 40.4

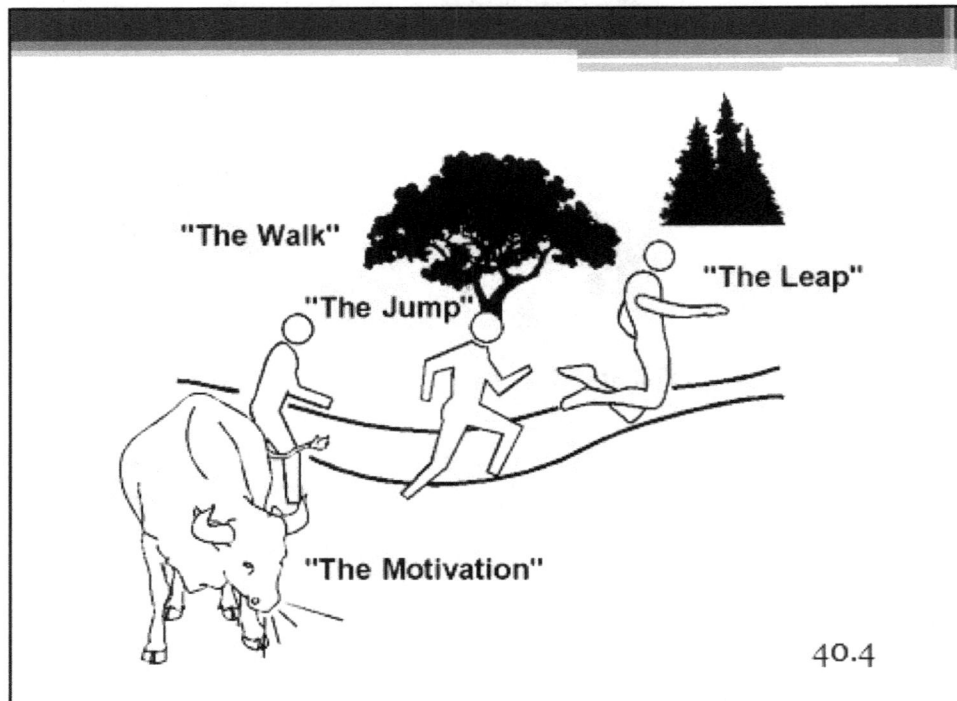

Part E.
Ethical Teamwork
Introduction: Kristin Arnold

Frank Bucaro, a professional speaker on ethics and values, defines ethics as "what you do when no one is looking." Ethics at the personal level is a conscious decision to do the "right thing"; however, on a team level, various team members may have different interpretations of what the right thing to do really is. Frank says, "Everybody speaks *their* truth, but it may not be *the* truth." I believe the very essence of teams and teamwork is to seek common ground and search for "the truth."

Gone unstated, individual team members create their own definitions of "the truth," what's right and wrong, as well as their own interpretations of proper standards of behavior. When operating from different truths, assumptions, and values, teams invariably are rife with conflict, behave badly, and are simply non-productive.

When team members are in alignment with the same values and standards, you don't have these kinds of problems. They are "open to each other's truths," as Frank says. Extraordinary teams work together to discover the truth, searching for common ground and building a consensus.

More importantly, they invest time to discuss and explicitly define their standards —or how they will work together to achieve "the truth." Some call these standards "ground rules," "guiding principles," or "team norms." They are explicit agreements on how the team will function. They clearly articulate boundaries of appropriate behavior. Effective ground rules *prevent* undesirable behaviors from happening in the first place. They also create a space to *intervene* gracefully— reminding each other of the prior agreements made.

As you formulate your ground rules, consider how your team will deal with common concerns such as:

- **Interruptions.** What to do when team members are called out of the meeting. How will you deal with phone calls and messages? Will pager and cellular phones be tolerated?

- **Assignments.** If team members cannot fulfill their obligations, who should they notify and by when?

245

- **Substitutions.** In the event a team member can't make it to the meeting, are "substitutions" allowed? How will the team's work be communicated to the missing team member?

- **Decisions.** How will the team make decisions? Are team members aiming for consensus? Is there a "fallback" in case the team can't come to a consensus? Is the team leader ultimately responsible for making the decision?

- **Confidentiality.** Are there topics or kinds of information that should not be discussed outside the team?

- **Penalties.** How will the team deal with minor and chronic violations to the ground rules?

Ground rules are simply the glue that holds the team together. Here's an example of one extraordinary team's ground rules:

- **Honor time limits.** Be on time. Start on time. End on time. Set a time frame for each deliverable. Do your part to meet individual and team commitments.

- **All participate... no one dominates.** Ask for ideas from everyone. Recognize and consider others' ideas. Accept all suggestions as valid for consideration.

- **Work together.** Team members communicate and work closely together and make every effort to support one another. Keep one another informed. Work together to solve problems. Offer help without being asked.

- **Listen as allies.** Give your undivided attention to the person speaking. Try to understand others first; second, try to be understood. Respect each other by not interrupting. Stay on track. Stick to the subject at hand. Minimize distractions and needless debate.

- **Be considerate.** Consider the background, motivations, and skills of other members when offering help or advice. Be open to constructive feedback.

- **Celebrate small successes.** Recognize team and individual effort.

- **Aim for consensus.** But if we cannot agree, we will park the issue on a "logjam" lot for a specified period of time.

- **Knock three times.** Simply knock your knuckle or a pen on the table three times if the discussion starts to wander or there is another minor violation of the ground rules. Whoever is speaking should stop and refocus on the topic.

- **Respect time and each other.**

It all boils down to this one last ground rule: respect each other. When you respect each other, it is much easier to discover the truth.

Submitted by: Kristin J. Arnold
48 West Queens Way
Hampton, VA 23669
Phone: 757-728-0191, 800-589-4733
Fax: 757-728-0192
E-mail: karnold@qpcteam.com
Web site: www.qpcteam.com

Kristin J. Arnold, CPCM, helps corporations, government, and nonprofit organizations achieve extraordinary results. With years of teambuilding and facilitation experience, Kristin specializes in coaching executives and their leadership, management, and employee teams, particularly in the areas of strategic, business and project planning, process improvement, decision-making, and collaborative problem-solving.

In addition to facilitation services, QPC, Inc., offers diversified programs around the team concept to meet the needs of CEOs, COOs, executives, managers, and team members. Her highly customized speeches and seminars are instrumental in achieving higher performance and results within the workplace.

41. Ethical Teamwork
Blindfold Obstacle Course

60 minutes plus 15 minutes pre- or post-lecturette

OVERVIEW
This exercise highlights the value of trustworthiness as it affects various roles and tactics team members use to deal with a perceived stressful situation. While the main activity may be made as easy or difficult as required, careful observation during the exercise and skillful facilitation by an experienced trainer during the debriefing is required. The exercise may be conducted in a large space, either indoors or outdoors.

PURPOSE
To develop awareness of the need for trust among team members.

GROUP SIZE
Any number may participate; participants will be divided into groups of eight members.

ROOM ARRANGEMENT
A large area (indoors or out) is required.

MATERIALS
- Blindfolds for each participating team member
- One rope per team long enough to tie each participant to other team members in a row with 2 to 3 feet of rope between each person
- Obstacles for the groups to go over, under, through, and/or around (see suggested obstacles at the end of instructions)
- Clipboards, observation sheets, and pencils for each observer

PROCEDURE
1. Divide participants into equal-sized groups, no larger than eight participants per group.
2. Assign one observer and one guide per group. Observers are responsible for completing the observation sheet and providing observations to the group during the activity debriefing. Guides are responsible for ensuring their assigned group completes the exercise safely. Each observer receives an observer sheet, clipboard, and pencil.

249

3. Give each group a rope and blindfold for every person. They are instructed to tie themselves together in a row, then place the blindfolds over their eyes so they are not able to see.

4. The guide from each group leads the group to their designated starting point and stays with them for the duration of the blindfold exercise. Guides tell their group what obstacle they are about to negotiate, e.g., a "water" obstacle, an "electric" fence, a rope hallway, etc.

5. The teams are given 5 minutes to negotiate the obstacles.

6. At the end of 5 minutes, the observer selects the team member who has been the least involved in the process to become the new guide. The original guide becomes a member of the blindfolded team. While still blindfolded, the team must reorder and retie themselves to include the new member.

7. The new group has 5 minutes to continue negotiating the remaining obstacles.

8. When the next 5-minute time frame is over, group members remove their blindfolds and untie themselves. Each group, including the observers and guides, gather around a flipchart and choose a scribe who writes the answers to the following questions:

   - Describe the experience in adjectives, e.g., "exciting," "scary," "frustrating."
   - What is the effect of trust involved in the activity on a team?
   - What did you learn about your team?
   - What did you learn about the roles each team member takes on?
   - What did you learn about the roles you take on within the team?

9. The Observer shares his or her observations after answers to the above questions are given.

10. Each group has a spokesperson to report answers to the larger group.

11. Based on the ideas shared, debrief the exercise from a larger viewpoint, identifying team issues raised; "food for thought" for participants' return to the workplace; and possible next steps toward establishing/maintaining their team. Discuss the obstacle course as a metaphor for workplace barriers and how teams must rely on one another to overcome these barriers.

12. Give a short lecturette on trust before or after the activity. Ideally, it will be given after the activity because more examples can be drawn to illustrate points made in step 8.

Suggested Obstacles

Inside Room
- Sturdy tables to go over, under, or through
- Ropes tied between solid stands to act as a "hallway" to follow
- Ropes tied between solid stands for teams to go under or to serve as "electric" fences
- Plastic sheets taped to the ground to signify water obstacles

Outside Room
- Sturdy tables, e.g., picnic tables to go over, under, or through
- Ropes tied between trees to act as a "hallway" to follow
- Ropes tied between trees for teams to go under or to serve as "electric" fences
- Actual water hazards, e.g., slow moving creeks, shallow ponds, puddles

Observation Sheets
- How did the team determine the order of the group when tying themselves together?
- How did team members determine who was the leader?
- What roles did the other team members take?
- Who gave the other team members verbal and physical assistance through the obstacles?
- Did the role of leader change throughout the exercise? If so, what caused the change?
- How did the team determine how to negotiate each obstacle?
- Did each group work collaboratively or competitively with other groups during the exercise? How did they determine if they were collaborative or competitive?
- What issues were raised during the exercise, e.g., trust, leadership, conflict?

Trust Lecturette

This portion of the activity is left to the discretion of the facilitator.

Trust is manifested in four ways:

Contract …you agree to do what you said you would do by shaking hands or signing a contract.

Competency …you have the capabilities to meet the competencies of the task.

Intentionality …you will fulfill your obligations (meet the goals and objectives) until the task is finished.

Depth …you will finish the task at a level consistent with what is defined as "good work" in relation to the task.

Through the activity:

1. What was the contract?

2. What were the competencies?

3. What intentions were associated with this activity?

4. What depth of completion was there?

5. Trustworthiness is realized through truthfulness or honesty, sincerity, candor, integrity, promise-keeping, loyalty. Of these principles, which were apparent in the activity?

These same questions can be asked in the workplace every day.

Submitted by: Stephen Hobbs, Ed.D., and Denise Dolph
WELLTH Learning Network
Calgary, Alberta, Canada, T2N 0Y3
Phone: (403) 252-8188
E-mail: info@wellthlearning.com
Web site: www.wellthlearning.com

Stephen Hobbs, Ed.D., is the creator of the WELLTH Learning Network, Inc., and co-founder of The International Institute for Cultural Transition, Inc., and the Cultural Transition Institute. His work experience includes manager, consultant, instructor, facilitator, theorist, and published author. His practice focuses on customized experience-based learning adventures for individuals, groups, and teams; culture and transition; workplace learning; and the manager as educator.

Denise Dolph is the president of Co-Creations, Inc., and is an associate of the WELLTH Learning Network. She is a seasoned human resources generalist with specialization in training and development, career consulting, and recruitment.

42. Ethical Teamwork
Duty in General

45 minutes

OVERVIEW
Several ethical issues are addressed in this team exercise, the foundation of which is the "general duty" clause of the Occupational Safety and Health Act (OSHA).

PURPOSE
To encourage discussion/action regarding the "duty" of colleagues to provide a safe work environment.

GROUP SIZE
Any size group. Participants will work in teams of six to eight participants.

ROOM ARRANGEMENT
If possible, round table groupings for team meetings.

MATERIALS
Flipchart and marking pens

PROCEDURE
1. Begin the assignment by presenting the following statistics:

   ✓ Homicide is the leading cause of death for women in the workplace, according to the U.S. Bureau of Labor Statistics. (For minority women, current or previous spouses or boyfriends were responsible for about 25 percent of the deaths.)

   ✓ According to the U.S. Department of Justice, approximately 10 percent of all absence from work is attributable to spousal abuse.

   ✓ Domestic abuse costs businesses nearly $5 billion a year.

2. Explain that employers can be found legally liable for domestic violence. OSHA contains a "general duty" clause that says employers must provide a workplace that protects workers from recognized hazards. An employee, then, whose husband came to her office and physically harmed her, might subsequently claim the employer was aware of her domestic problems and failed to protect her.

3. Point out, too, that one of the recommendations for taking protective steps is the establishment of a post-violent-incident team. According to *HR Manager's Legal Reporter*, this team has the following duties:

   ✓ To deal with victims, employees, survivors, and others affected by a violent incident immediately after it occurs.

   ✓ To assign qualified team members duties dealing with security, medical care, and supervisory/managerial responsibilities that follow in the wake of such an incident.

4. Form teams of six to eight members. They are to assume their management is concerned enough about the "general duty" clause that they would like this team to determine:

   ✓ How safe their environment really is from domestic violence spillover.

   ✓ Who would serve on the post-violent-incident team and what their duties would be.

   ✓ If the team would be ethically correct in approaching several minority women whom the team suspects may be in physical danger.

5. Debrief on two levels:

   Content: How valuable was the team's output? (Specify the forces that worked to achieve and to prevent accomplishment.)

   Context: How well did this team function as a team? (Note the items in the Variation section.)

VARIATION

Appoint observers who will determine if:

   ✓ The team wasted time.
   ✓ A leader was appointed.
   ✓ An agenda was used. (If so, it should be clearly written on the flipchart, with time allocations listed for each item.)
   ✓ A time monitor was appointed.
   ✓ A topic monitor was appointed.
   ✓ The team accomplished its goal.
   ✓ The meeting began with a re-statement/clarification of purpose.
   ✓ Team members stayed on target.

Ask the observers to prepare a general report ("There was one instance when a person appeared argumentative..." rather than "Phyllis just wouldn't let go of her viewpoint.") and to share it with the group at large.

DISCUSSION

- Under what circumstances do we have the right to interfere in a co-worker's private life?

- How safe is your work environment?

- Is there a policy related to domestic violence and its transference to the workplace?

- If so, what procedure does it specify? How widely is that procedure known?

- If not, what could you do to create such a policy?

QUOTATION

"Give what you have. To someone, it may be better than you dare think."
– Henry Wadsworth Longfellow

POINTS OF INTEREST

An additional liability for employers lies in negligence demonstrated by hiring, retaining, or supervising an employee who winds up hurting someone on the job. If the injured person can show the employer knew or should have known that the perpetrator was not suited for the job and that his or her actions could predictably lead to violence, the injured party would probably win the lawsuit.

43. Ethical Teamwork
Judgment Daze

Approximately 45 minutes

OVERVIEW
Teams discuss their reasons for selecting possible courses of action related to actual work-related cases. The team(s) that most often rules the way the judge ruled is awarded a token prize.

PURPOSE
To apprise participants of legal outcomes that may prevent them from engaging in unlawful, if not unethical, behavior.

GROUP SIZE
Any size group will work, as long as teams can be formed with the same number of participants in each.

ROOM ARRANGEMENT
Seating that will accommodate teams working around a table.

MATERIALS
- Handouts 43.1 through 43.5, *"Court Shorts,"* for each participant
- **Optional:** Token prizes for the winning team, such as miniature gavels or simply pieces of fruit or already-read books about teamwork

PROCEDURES
1. Discuss the fact that laws are broken sometimes by people who are absolutely unaware that the laws they are breaking even exist. Because teams are so integral a part of corporate life, team members may in fact be unaware of some laws that could directly affect them.

2. Present an overview of the assignment: Teams will discuss workplace situations involving teams and team members and will come to decisions regarding the "right" course of action. The team that has the most right answers will emerge victorious and will be so recognized (if only through applause).

3. Divide the group into teams with an equal number of participants in each.

4. Distribute the first handout and allow the teams 5 minutes to complete it.

5. Continue with each of the remaining handouts.

6. Share the answers:

   1 = False. If such remarks are made in the presence of employees likely to take offense at such statements, Ken may be guilty of unlawful harassment.

   2 = True. But an employee who claimed he had taped conversations without telling people just to refresh his memory had to pay co-workers and his company $132,000.

   3 = True (assuming this was not a singular example). In the actual case, a New York City bank had to pay the employee $2,600,000.

   4 = True. The law firm in the actual case had to pay a $6,900,000 fine and the attorney himself (who was also guilty of touching the employee and making lewd remarks) was fined $225,000.

   5 = False. The court found "the First Amendment is not a license for interference with the proper functioning of the workplace." The court also denied the discrimination claim as the company was able to prove its policies applied to everyone.

7. Award recognition and possibly token prizes to the winning team(s).

VARIATION
Invite someone from the legal department of the participants' organization (or another organization) to discuss labor and employment laws.

DISCUSSION
- What is the worst legal mistake you can make at work?
- What functions, once performed only by managers, are now being handled by teams?
- How much responsibility does/should your organization assume in making employees aware of labor and employment laws?

QUOTATION
"Leadership is a potent combination of strategy and character. But if you must be without one, be without the strategy."
  – General H. Norman Schwarzkopf

POINTS OF INTEREST

When infractions have occurred, it's the team leader's or supervisor's responsibility to provide coaching feedback to the person who may have committed the infraction. The following questions will help during coaching sessions:

1. Is there a real infraction or simply hearsay evidence of such?

2. Have standards been made clear to the individual before the incident?

3. Can you assume the correct behavior would be "obvious" to any reasonable person?

4. Has such behavior been tolerated in the past?

5. Has tolerance of the behavior been accepted in the past depending on the individual, the group, the task, and the situation?

6. Will you be able to maintain your objectivity in this investigation?

7. What resources do you need to call on?

8. Should there be a suspension period for the employee while the investigation is ongoing?

9. Have you given the employee an opportunity to present his or her version of the event?

10. What disciplinary precedents are there?

11. What does the employee's previous record tell you?

12. Could the contemplated action be considered discriminatory?

13. What documentation is required? How much time is needed to resolve this issue?

14. What possible repercussions could be harmful to others? To the organization itself?

Handout 43.1
Court Shorts

Situation

James, Ken, Cynthia, Robert, and Phyllis serve on a cross-functional team, the purpose of which is to survey employees to learn why retention rates are lower than the industry norm. They've finally finished compiling the survey results and have decided to celebrate by having dinner together. Just as they're about to leave work for the restaurant, Cynthia receives a call advising that her teen-age son has broken his ankle in football practice. She gives her regrets at not being able to celebrate with her team and heads home.

During the dinner, Cynthia's name comes up and the team leader, Ken, moves from a discussion of how pleasant Cynthia is to how sexy she is. Because he is out of the office, it's after working hours, and Cynthia is not present, it is perfectly acceptable for him to express his opinion.

True or False?

Handout 43.2
Court Shorts

Situation

Sam was the first to acknowledge the team meetings were not going as smoothly as he had hoped. The problem was, when he sat down to analyze what went wrong, he had forgotten most of what was said. At the next team meeting, he advises his team that he's planning to tape record the meeting in an attempt to better understand the problem. Because he obtained their consent beforehand, it is perfectly legal to tape record the proceedings.

True or False?

Reproduced from *50 Reproducible Activities for Promoting Ethics Within the Organization*, by Marlene Caroselli. HRD Press, 2015.

Handout 43.3
Court Shorts

Situation

Roberto often brings Italian pastries to team meetings—his brother owns a pastry shop. As the team gathers around the coffee and cannolis, they often make remarks such as, *"This is an offer I can't refuse."* Although he makes an important contribution to the work of the team, he has not impressed his boss as much as he has impressed his teammates. His boss fires him with accusations that he created a "Mafia shop." The boss also explained during the termination meeting that he needed "a true American" who could deal with external customers.

Roberto sues on the basis of discrimination against national origin and will likely win.

True or False?

Reproduced from *50 Reproducible Activities for Promoting Ethics Within the Organization*, by Marlene Caroselli. HRD Press, 2015.

Handout 43.4
Court Shorts

Situation

Although Quentin's team is known for getting the job done, they're also known for having a good time as they do so. They often horse around with one another before the meeting starts. Joe, who provides legal counsel for the project they're implementing, is one of the most mischievous team members. He playfully dropped candy one morning in the blouse pocket of Harriette, a new addition to the team. He tapped her on the arm and told her not to worry, he wasn't planning to take the candy back. Harriette has sufficient grounds for a lawsuit.

True or False?

Handout 43.5
Court Shorts

Situation

Elijah is a born-again Christian who holds Bible study meetings with his team before they start their regular meetings. He had his secretary type notes from both the Bible study meetings and the regular meetings. The secretary, not part of the team, complained and Elijah was asked to stop using company resources for religious activities. He complied and even went so far as to remove all religious materials from his office.

Not long afterward, Elijah was fired for poor performance. He sued on the basis of race and religion and a violation of his Constitutional right to free speech. He will probably win the case.

True or False?

Reproduced from *50 Reproducible Activities for Promoting Ethics Within the Organization*, by Marlene Caroselli. HRD Press, 2015.

44. Ethical Teamwork
Information Age-ing

Approximately 10 minutes

OVERVIEW
Team leaders work hard to establish an environment that is casual, open, and relaxed. However, if that environment allows or—worse yet, encourages—age-related comments, an organization may be liable for violations of the Age Discrimination in Employment Act (ADEA). This exercise asks participants to compile a list of phrases that team members might innocently use in reference to older employees—phrases that *could* serve as the basis for subsequent lawsuits.

PURPOSE
To sharpen awareness of casual phrases that could lead to charges of age discrimination.

GROUP SIZE
Any size group. Participants will meet in small groups.

ROOM ARRANGEMENT
No special arrangement required other than seating that permits easy group formation.

MATERIALS
- Flipchart and marking pens
- Masking tape

PROCEDURE
1. Introduce the exercise by reviewing the Points of Interest.

2. Divide the class into small groups and distribute a sheet of flipchart paper and a marking pen to each.

3. Ask them to write phrases such as "Young Turks" and others that, however innocent their original intention, may in fact produce subsequent legal difficulty.

4. Have a spokesperson from each group come forward and hang the list on the wall. As he or she reviews the items on the list, ask the other groups to cross off any duplicates on their own lists.

5. Continue to have each group send a spokesperson forward to review the phrases.

6. Debrief with a reminder that teams are expected to do more than accomplish their mission. They are also expected to accomplish that mission in a safe and respectful environment.

VARIATION

Prepare a script ahead of time for a team leader and a team member. The script should have several phrases that could be viewed as discriminatory, such as, *"Are you thinking about retirement?"* Have two volunteers enact the script in a fishbowl setting while the remaining participants take note of the potentially dangerous comments.

DISCUSSION

- How uncomfortable does it make you to know that simple phrases like "you can't teach an old dog new tricks" could be used in an age-discrimination lawsuit?

- What kinds of ethical guidelines should a team leader establish at the first team meeting?

- How old do you have to be to receive protection from ADEA? (**Answer:** 40 or older.)

QUOTATION

"Age is a question of mind over matter. If you don't mind, it don't matter."
— LeRoy Satchel Paige

POINTS OF INTEREST

In Buffalo, New York, a 48-year-old salesman for a steel company was awarded nearly $1 million in damages when he claimed his dismissal was the result of age discrimination and not the result of poor work performance or even customer complaints as the company charged. Included in the evidence he offered was the fact that rising stars were often called "young tigers" by his manager.

A 64-year-old Missouri school bus driver used the phrase "old enough to retire" to help convince a jury she was discharged for age discrimination and not speeding, as the company claimed. Further proof was her supervisor's comment at her birthday party: he told her he "didn't know that she was that old." The jury awarded her $76,000 in damages.

45. Ethical Teamwork
Whistle-Blown in the Wind

Approximately 20 minutes

OVERVIEW

Based on real-world situations, this exercise has participants selecting one of several courses of action and discussing their selection with a partner.

PURPOSE

- To develop recognition that there are several choices possible in virtually any situation.
- To discuss possible courses of action to be taken when legal, moral, and/or ethical violations have occurred.

GROUP SIZE

Any size group. Participants will first work alone on a handout and will then discuss their answers with others who've made the same choices.

ROOM ARRANGEMENT

If possible, table groups for four or five participants.

MATERIALS

- Equipment for displaying PowerPoint slides
- Slide 45.1, *"Laws to Protect"*
- Handout 45.1, *"Whistle-Blown in the Wind"*
- **Optional:** Token prizes of some sort for the winning team

PROCEDURE

1. Ask participants what they know about whistle-blowing and the laws that protect those who uncover and disclose unethical or illegal practices.

2. Display Slide 45.1, *"Laws to Protect"* and briefly discuss each law, using the Points of Interest provided by the Bureau of Business Practice.

3. Distribute Handout 45.1, *Whistle-Blown in the Wind"* and ask participants to work on it alone and then to discuss their answers with a partner.

4. Arrange for further discussion by arranging subgroups as follows: those who had answers (a) and (a) will form one team. The same will be done for those with answers (a) and (b); (a) and (c); and (a) and (d). A fifth group will be composed of those who had any other combination.

5. The larger groups will continue the discussion of their choices, bringing in personal experience whenever possible.

6. Share the real-world outcome of this scenario—(a) and (b)—and recognize the winning team with a token prize or with a call to their managers, commending their insight.

7. Debrief by sharing the court's decision: They upheld the discharge, maintaining that foul language and disrespectful conduct were sufficient reasons for the firing. The whistle-blowing wasn't the real issue here: behavior was.

VARIATION
Have subgroups prepare a list of recommended steps for employees to follow when they discover deliberate or inadvertent wrongdoing. Make a similar list for managers to follow once the wrongdoing is reported.

DISCUSSION
- How protected are you at work?

- Do you think new hires should be made aware of these protections as part of their orientation? Explain.

- Have you ever been asked a question during a job interview that was illegal? If so, what did you do? Why did you choose this course of action?

QUOTATION
"Time is a dressmaker specializing in alterations."
                                            – Faith Baldwin

POINTS OF INTEREST
False Claims Act: Whistle-blowers may receive up to 25 percent of the amount the federal government recovers from contractors who have committed fraud. The government is actually allowed triple damages. The use of this act is spreading to comparable situations in Medicare billing.

Industry-specific laws: Within given business arenas, laws exist to protect those who blow the whistle on companies engaged in unsafe practices.

OSHA: Under the provisions of this law, employers must create and maintain a workplace that does not jeopardize health or safety. Employees who report unsafe conditions are protected under the act.

NLRA: Union activities are protected under this law, and employers who attempt to prevent or stop such activities are guilty of unfair labor practice. They could be taken to court for these actions.

Title VII and ADEA: Workers who report discriminatory hiring questions or discriminatory statements/actions while employed are protected by these laws.

State laws: In some states, employees who lose their job for reporting violations can file a lawsuit and would probably emerge victorious. Further, protections are offered in many states for those who blow the whistle on private-sector infractions.

Slide 45.1

Laws to Protect

The False Claims Act

Industry-specific laws

The Occupational Safety and Health Act (OSHA)

The National Labor Relations Act (NLRA)

Title VII and Age Discrimination in Employment Act (ADEA)

State laws

45.1

Handout 45.1
Whistle-Blown in the Wind

Scenario

Mark is an inspection team leader. His people have been reporting defects to management for weeks now and nothing has been done. Mark finally insisted that the quality manager attend their team meeting, figuring there would be considerably more strength in numbers for the manager to hear. Nils showed up and is taking a somewhat defensive stance: *"Now don't get belligerent about this,"* he placated. *"I'm sure we can work it out."*

"Forget working it out," Mark's voice rose. *"You've known about this for a month now and nothing's been done."* Mark continued, becoming more angered as he cataloged the problems and heard supporting comments from his team. He literally got "in the face" of the manager. The arguments escalated until Mark threatened to quit, emphasizing his point with profanity.

"No need to quit," Nils shouted. *"I'm firing you for insubordination."*

What do you think Nils did? (Contemplate what you would have done.)

    (a) Stood by his decision and took the necessary post-firing steps to ensure Mark was officially terminated.
    (b) Offered a three-day suspension instead of firing.
    (c) Arranged a counseling session with Mark, the HR director, and himself.
    (d) Asked the team as a whole for a written report of the defects problem.

What do you think Mark did? (Consider what you would have done.)

    (a) Asked for a mediator to be present at the team meeting with Nils.
    (b) Go to court, claiming the firing was in retaliation for whistle-blowing.
    (c) Apologize and ask to be reinstated.
    (d) Ask for a transfer to a different department.

Reproduced from *50 Reproducible Activities for Promoting Ethics Within the Organization*, by Marlene Caroselli. HRD Press, 2015.

46. Ethical Teamwork
How Do You Spell "L-E-A-D-E-R"?

Approximately 20 minutes

OVERVIEW
More in the nature of an energizer than ethical analysis, this exercise elicits consideration of the qualities necessary for ethical team leadership.

PURPOSE
- To develop awareness of the traits possessed by effective team leaders.
- To evaluate the pros and cons of charisma for a team leader.

GROUP SIZE
Any size group can participate in this exercise: they will work in pairs and then in quartets. (**Note:** If the total number of participants is not divisible by four, simply form small groups of three to five participants.)

ROOM ARRANGEMENT
No special arrangement required.

MATERIALS
- Handout 46.1, *"How Do You Spell L-E-A-D-E-R?"*
- Flipchart and marking pens

PROCEDURE
1. Begin by pointing out that the topic of leadership has been explored for thousands of years. Numerous studies have been undertaken to determine exactly what qualities leaders possess. Ask for some descriptors of leaders and record them on the flipchart.

2. Post the list and start a second list by asking, "Which of these words also apply to team leaders?" After recording several, ask, "Which words not already mentioned do you feel are important for team leaders to have?"

3. Divide the group into pairs and ask each pair to select one word from either list and relate it to team leaders they've known in the past.

4. Ask each pair to join one other pair to discuss their observations.

5. Distribute Handout 46.1, *"How Do You Spell L-E-A-D-E-R?"* Ask the two-pair teams to identify the word many would associate with effective leadership—whether it's leadership of a team or any other group. (The answer is "charisma.")

6. Recognize the first team to finish by a round of applause.

7. Conclude with a discussion of the positive and negative aspects of charismatic leadership. Use the Discussion questions, the Quotation, and the Points of Interest as a guide.

VARIATION

Encourage participants who actually serve as team leaders to distribute a small sheet of paper to each team member at their next team meeting. Ask each person to anonymously write a one-word answer to this question: *"What do you think is my best quality as your team leader?"* Encourage the leaders to analyze the answers after the meeting and profit from the honesty contained within.

DISCUSSION

*   What's the worst trait a team leader could possess?

*   What traits do you exemplify when you lead meetings?

*   In a team composed of high-powered personalities, what trait is the most important for the team leader to demonstrate?

*   Think about the best teams you've ever been part of. Is there a particular quality the leaders of those teams had in common? If so, what is it?

*   Think about the worst teams you've ever been part of. What quality did the meeting leaders have in common?

*   Is it possible for a leader to develop a charismatic personality?

*   If you believe it is possible, how do you feel about the ethics of a decision to become (more) charismatic?

*   What words would you use to define the word "charisma"?

QUOTATION

"Besides intelligence and a knack for strategic planning, they [good managers/leaders] have enormous charm and energy. They have charisma."
                                                        – Robert Hogan

POINTS OF INTEREST

Psychologist Robert Hogan of the Tulsa Institute of Behavioral Sciences has conducted research involving thousands of managers. He acknowledges there can be a dark side, though, to charisma. Basically, it's the difference between healthy narcissism and unhealthy narcissism. Among the negatives associated with destructive charismatic leaders are behaviors like these among followers:

- ✓ A tendency to groupthink because it's safer than being a devil's advocate.

- ✓ A strong desire to please the leader, even if it means altering the truth.

- ✓ A feeling of discomfort or pressure in the presence of the unhealthy narcissist.

- ✓ Few attempts at levity.

Handout 46.1
How Do You Spell L-E-A-D-E-R?

Directions
In each of the eight lines below, one letter of the alphabet is missing. Once you discover what it is, write it in the blank line to the right of the letters. Once you've written all eight letters in a vertical line, you'll have the trait many consider important for a team leader to possess.

1. QLXATFYGRNUDPIWBZVWSJHEKO   _____

2. XFAZBULPLWCJGVNYRDEISKTQM   _____

3. KNYCOJDPEYTUSFQZGLVHIWTMX   _____

4. IAQBFCLWJEUSKGDMXZTNOVYHP   _____

5. AGBCJDPERKZMQOUVFWSXTYJHN   _____

6. ZAFBTPDQEJKHLMGNOUVDRWXYC   _____

7. FDSGCHOQLUKVIXNJPQYWRESBZA   _____

8. ZKGLQJBMCEFNOURVHSWPIEXDT   _____

47. Ethical Teamwork
Declarations of Dependence

Approximately 15 minutes

OVERVIEW
This fun exercise reminds participants of the dangers associated with a leader's decision to make overreaching, self-aggrandizing statements.

PURPOSE
To highlight the damage that can be caused (to one's image as well as to the organization itself) through overly strong assertions.

MATERIALS
- Handout 47.1, *"Declarations of Dependence"*
- **Optional:** Two truth-detector awards, such as copies of mysteries or true crime stories.

GROUP SIZE
Any size group can engage in this exercise.

ROOM ARRANGEMENT
A U-shaped formation works well for this exercise.

PROCEDURE
1. Begin with a brief discussion of the importance of having a focus, a purpose, a goal—not only for a given team meeting but also for the long-term project of which a particular team meeting is just one part.

2. Tell participants you are going to distribute a list of statements (Handout 47.1, *"Declarations of Dependence"*) made—or *not* made—by famous people, many of whom served in a leadership capacity. While we have no way of knowing whether or not they were with their teams when the statements were made, we do know that declarative statements like these can either be a source of inspiration ... or ridicule. They can bespeak our dependence on one another as team members or they can be so embarrassing they virtually isolate us from others. To be avoided are the loose-cannon statements, the opinions so radical they cause the speaker to be regarded as a spokesperson for no one else but him- or herself. Not only can loose-cannon statements mislead followers, they can, on occasion, be unethical in their usurping of power.

3. Ask participants to pair off and work with the person next to them. Tell them their job is to determine if the statements on the handout were truly made by the person listed beside the statement. Point out that with one possible exception, each of these individuals were in positions of power.

    (**Answers:** 1–Yes, 2–Yes, 3–No, 4–Yes, 5–Yes, 6–Yes, 7–Yes, 8–Yes, 9–No, 10–No)

    Consider awarding a Truth-Detector prize to the first pair to get eight or more answers correct.

4. Conclude by asking new pairs to decide if the handout statements showed power wisely used—if only the power of attracting the press. Then, have them create a single sentence that a team leader could use to make a strong assertion about the team's purpose at the very first team meeting. The sentence should reflect strength and leadership, power and determination—but not at the expense of team harmony. Call on each pair to share their statement and comment on the seeming use or abuse of power suggested by each.

VARIATION

Obtain a copy of a speech delivered by a well-known individual—the organization's CEO, for example, or the president of the United States. Analyze it for phrases that suggest power but not an unethical abuse of power. Apply the analysis to any programs dealing with Leadership, Communications, or Persuasion.

DISCUSSION

- Think about the last meeting you attended. Did the meeting leader make an overarching statement that alluded to purpose/outcome and that also helped develop the sense of dependence on one another, necessary for achieving that outcome?

- Can you think of some famous historical statements (such as Franklin Delano Roosevelt's *"The only thing we have to fear is fear itself"*) that speak of a need for a collective commitment in order to survive and succeed?

- What statements (organizational or national) have you known to backfire— statements such as Alexander Haig's infamous *"I'm in charge here!"* asserted immediately after the shooting of President Reagan.

- How would you describe the statements that inspire groups? (For example, most of them are short statements.)

QUOTATION

"One can never consent to creep when one feels an impulse to soar."
– Helen Keller

POINTS OF INTEREST

The following checklist from *The Language of Leadership* is specifically geared to "The Language of Power."

_____ Am I using power-words in my spoken and written communications? (A power phrase would be the definite "Three o'clock," as opposed to the squishy "Threeish.")

_____ Do I continually apologize?

_____ Do I overexplain things?

_____ Do I use imperative sentences?

_____ Have I used a format to illustrate my points when appropriate?

_____ Do I waste other people's time?

_____ Do I use facts to substantiate my points?

_____ Do I show an orderly expression of my ideas?

_____ Do I employ anecdotes as appropriate?

_____ Do I have variety in my sentence structure?

_____ Do I avoid unnecessary repetition?

_____ Could anything I've said come back to haunt me?

_____ Do I use the active rather than the passive voice?

Handout 47.1
Declarations of Dependence

Directions
Words are the team leader's best friend, for they help him or her establish purpose, keep meetings on target, and achieve intended outcomes. However, carelessly framed ideas and thoughtlessly expressed words can do just the opposite. Your job is to determine if the person next to the quote actually spoke these words. Write **"true"** or **"false"** in the blank space in front of each.

_____ 1. "I'm just here for the drugs." – Nancy Reagan

_____ 2. "Life is indeed precious, and I believe the death penalty helps to affirm this fact." – Ed Koch, former NYC mayor

_____ 3. "Mad cow disease is a uniquely European problem and should be uniquely solved by the Europeans themselves." – General Colin Powell

_____ 4. "The reason so many people showed up at Louis B. Mayer's funeral was because they wanted to make sure he was dead." – Samuel Goldwyn

_____ 5. "Kevin Costner is like Oakland: There is no there there." – Marcello Mastroianni

_____ 6. "Bo Derek turned down the role of Helen Keller because she couldn't remember the lines." – Joan Rivers

_____ 7. "I have known many meat eaters to be far more nonviolent than vegetarians." – Mahatma Gandhi

_____ 8. "Health food may be good for the conscience, but Oreos taste a hell of a lot better." – Robert Redford

_____ 9. "There are no secret vices, especially not when it comes to gluttony." – George W. Bush

_____ 10. "Washington is the only place in the world where a person can get stabbed in the back while climbing a ladder." – Linda Tripp

48. Ethical Teamwork
There Is No Terror

Approximately 25 minutes

OVERVIEW
In this exercise, participants have an opportunity to learn how team leaders can help drive out specific fears via specific actions.

PURPOSE
- To explore one cause of fear in the workplace.
- To better understand the ethical and unethical approaches to dealing with fear.

GROUP SIZE
Any size group. Participants will first work alone, then as an entire group, and finally in small groups.

ROOM ARRANGEMENT
No special arrangement required.

MATERIALS
- Flipchart and marking pens
- Equipment for displaying PowerPoint slides
- Slide 48.1, *"There Is No Terror"*

PROCEDURE
1. Begin by asking participants to think of the worst thing they have ever done, something they wouldn't want others in the group to know. (If you sense some may be uncomfortable, you can lighten the mood a bit by suggesting, "It may be the time you ate a whole chocolate cake by yourself and pretended to know nothing about its disappearance, or the time you dressed as Elvis, then drove your teenager to the mall and identified yourself to mall-walkers as the teen's parent.")

2. After a few minutes, assure them they won't be asked to share their misdeeds but that you'd like to know how they felt when they thought they might have to. To encourage input, show Slide 48.1, *"There Is No Terror,"* and lead a brief discussion of Alfred Hitchcock's observation, *"There is no terror in the bang, only in the anticipation of it."* List the tension-related feelings on a sheet of flipchart paper.

3. Segue to a discussion of how these and other negative feelings (especially fear of the unknown) can impact team effectiveness if they are not resolved in some way. Explain that when a team leader is just forming a group or when a leader of any kind is secretive and others don't know "where he or she is coming from," the resulting tension can seriously impact morale and output as well. Extend discussion, if possible, to the question of trust, and what happens when national leaders make revelations that erode that trust.

   Explore, too, the concept of "silo-ism," employed by unethical leaders who keep knowledge in and keep people out. Such individuals believe that knowledge is power and the more knowledge they can keep to themselves, the more power they will have.

4. Assign one or two of the negative, tension-related feelings to each table group. Have them discuss ways a team leader can determine causes of fear or tension and how they can best be dealt with by an ethical leader. Ask each group to reduce their discussion to a single sentence, ideally a memorable one, such as Bruce Tuckman's description of the stages of team formation: "Form, Storm, Norm, Perform."

   Groups can prepare their report using techniques other than rhyme, of course. They can employ alliteration, cleverness, numbers, letters (such as the ABC's of Fear-Removal), and even "chiasmus." This is a literary device that takes words from the first half of the sentence and gives them a new meaning, form, or twist in the second half. For example, Vincent Van Gogh once described the artistic process in this way: *"First I dream the painting. Then I paint the dream."*

VARIATION
Icebreaker: To help reduce the fear team members naturally bring to their first team meeting, ask each member this question and have them write down their answers: "In relation to work, what lights your fire?" Once they've finished, ask next, "In relation to work, what burns you up?" Again, have them record their answers. Go around the table and ask each person to share his or her first answer. (Allow input from others if they are so inclined.) Record the work activities that "light their fires." You can use these later when making assignments, e.g., assign data-analysis to the person who likes to "crunch numbers," rather than to the individual with a more creative bent.

Conclude this introductory exercise by asking each team member what bothers him or her. Make note of these answers as well, to avoid future embarrassment or transgressions. The individual who, for example, is angered when his or her integrity is questioned, requires delicately posed questions. The individual who resents micromanagement will need a freer rein than others will. Respecting individuals and their unique personalities lies at the heart of ethical treatment of others.

DISCUSSION

- Recall a time when someone took advantage of you by exploiting a fear you have.

- What is the worst error someone on your team could make?

- How can team leaders best handle the aftermath of mistakes team members might make?

- What connections can you make between fear and rumors?

QUOTATION

"Avoiding danger is no safer in the long run than outright exposure. Life is either a daring adventure, or nothing."

– Helen Keller

POINTS OF INTEREST

Tom Peters (and numerous other experts) acknowledge mistakes as a normal part of ultimate success. Says Peters, "Mistakes are not the 'spice' of life. Mistakes are life. Mistakes are not to be tolerated. They are to be encouraged. (And, mostly, the bigger the better.)"

Team leaders can help reduce the fear of mistakes and their consequences by sharing the procedure that will be employed should a mistake be made. This is the procedure recommended by Ernest Fair:

1. Uncover causes carefully.
2. Reexamine operating procedure.
3. Apply a mistake's solution to other areas of your business.
4. Examine any recent changes in routine.
5. Remember your shortcomings.

Slide 48.1

"There Is No Terror"

"There is no terror in the bang, only in the anticipation of it."

— Alfred Hitchcock

48.1

49. Ethical Teamwork
This Is the House That MAC Built

Approximately 20 minutes

OVERVIEW
Through the use of puzzle pieces labeled "M," "A," or "C," participants form three groups of words (beginning with their assigned letter) that reflect or *don't* reflect ethical teamwork.

PURPOSE
- To enhance a collaborative spirit.
- To analyze the elements of ethical teamwork.

GROUP SIZE
Any size group, to be divided into three subgroups.

ROOM ARRANGEMENT
No special arrangement required.

MATERIALS
- Flipchart and marking pens
- Puzzle pieces
- **Optional:** Token prizes such as inexpensive puzzles for each subgroup member

PROCEDURE
1. Before class begins, draw a simple house on a rectangular sheet of paper (11 x 17 inches works well) and divide it into three even columns, as shown on the next page. (**Note:** You can choose to make your design more sophisticated—if you have artistic talent or if you wish to cut out a picture of a house and glue it on to a large piece of cardboard. Just be sure to keep it on a rectangle and follow the same instructions.) Color one column red; the next blue; and the last green. Cut the paper into three columns. Then cut each column into puzzle pieces. The pieces from the first column should all have the letter "M" written on the back. The pieces from the second column should all have the letter "A" written on the back. And the pieces from the third column should all have the letter "C" written on the back.

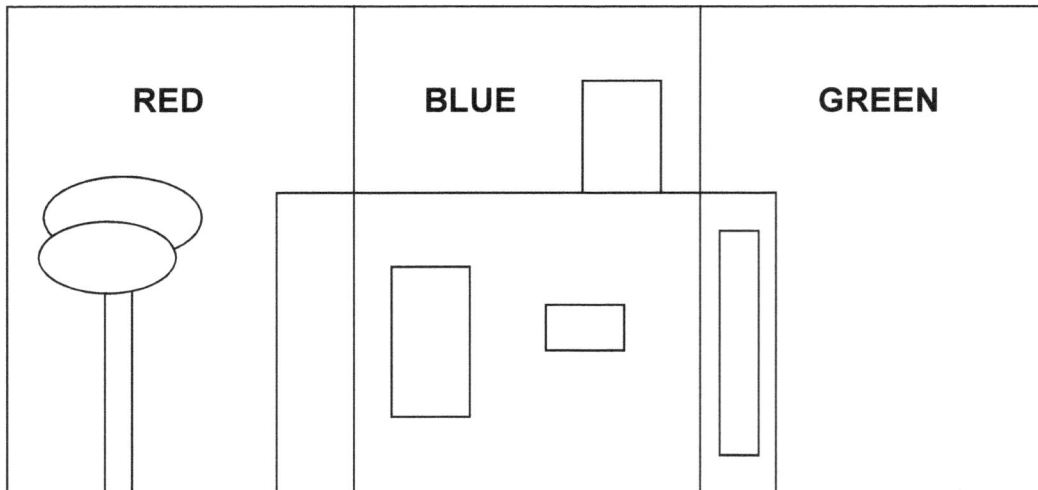

RED	BLUE	GREEN

2. Distribute the pieces. Ask all those with a puzzle piece that has an "M" on the back to form one group. Ask those holding "A" pieces to form a second group, and those with "C" pieces to form a third.

3. Give all three groups this assignment: "You now have 5 minutes to list all the words you can think of that start with the letter 'M,' 'A,' or 'C'—depending on the group you are in. These words must pertain to ethical teamwork or… to the opposite of ethical teamwork. Examples for the 'M' group might be 'maximization (of team potential)' and, on the negative side, 'manipulation.'"

4. After 5 minutes, ask which group had the longest list. Award the token prizes, if you wish, and then ask a spokesperson to explain each of the words on the list.

5. Bring closure by asking a volunteer from each of the three teams to gather all the pieces and to complete the whole puzzle. As they do so, you can call on the other two teams to share some of their words. Once the puzzle is complete, declare, "This is the house that MAC built. Remember that, in any team effort, the sum is truly greater than any or all of the parts. The more you use the ethical 'M,' 'A,' and 'C' words we've identified, the more likely you are to achieve the results you desire."

VARIATION
Ask for a volunteer committee to create actual banners or single-word posters that can be mounted in meeting rooms to encourage cooperative, ethical teambuilding.

Encourage others to do a weekly e-mail single-paragraph newsletter (with their manager's approval). The mailing will deal with one of the positive "M," "A," or "C" words each week.

DISCUSSION

- In your own experience, what is the best way to achieve harmony in a team?

- What unethical behaviors can lead to dysfunctional teams?

- Why or how do team members have a moral obligation to work together?

QUOTATION

"The road uphill and the road downhill are one and the same."

– Heraclitus

POINTS OF INTEREST

The National Institute of Business Management, in an article titled "The Politics of Teamwork," encourages cooperation through the avoidance of "trickery, misdirection and gamesmanship." You can acquire the information you require, the Institute asserts, without being unethical. How? By being straightforward. There's a danger in assuming cooperation won't be extended, in assuming games have to be played. Find someone in the organization you trust, someone who may have information your team needs to proceed, and simply ask for what you need. Even if the individual is not in a position to share that information with you, his or her body language, pauses, and vocal intonations may give you clues that could be valuable. The Institute also recommends calling in favors when there is something your team must have in order to achieve its goal. Cooperation is, after all, built on the gives and takes, the yin and yang, the ebb and tide of relationships.

50. Ethical Teamwork
Story Glory

Approximately 45 minutes

OVERVIEW
Participants first take a quiz and then think of a story illustrating an ethical situation that evoked a team's respect (or lack thereof) for their team leader or their manager. The stories are then shared and voted on. One storyteller from each group regales other groups with the story.

PURPOSE
- To encourage the use of storytelling as a convincing form of communication.
- To use stories to illustrate ethical team-related behaviors.

GROUP SIZE
Any size group. Participants will first work alone and then in four small groups.

ROOM ARRANGEMENT
No special arrangement required other than seating flexible enough to accommodate the formation of four small groups (up to eight plus participants in each if the class is especially large).

MATERIALS
- Handout 50.1, *"Teaming by Storying Around"*
- Small scraps of paper—one for each participant
- **Optional:** A token prize such as a book of short stories for the best storyteller

PROCEDURE
1. Begin by asking participants to think about an extremely ethical team leader (or leader of a management team) they've known in their past work experience. Then ask them to think of a story that illustrates that person's ethical behavior. Ask them to make a note or two about the story and tell them you'll be using the stories at a later time.

2. Distribute Handout 50.1 and allow 5 to 10 minutes for participants to complete it. Then, share the answers: 1. (a), 2. (d), 3. (g).

3. Divide the class into small groups of three to five participants. Ask them to share in turn their stories regarding an ethical action taken by the leader of a workplace team.

4. Once each person has told his or her story in the small group, ask the group to decide on the story that (1) best illustrates an ethical precept and (2) was most dramatically conveyed.

5. Have the storyteller in each group whose story was voted most dramatically illustrative move to another table and share his or her story with that group. The chosen storyteller from that table will be at another table, sharing his or her story. Continue with the rotations until each of the four table groups has had a chance to hear three other stories (in addition to their own).

6. Distribute small scraps of paper and ask each person to write the name of the storyteller he or she felt had the "best" story, in terms of making an ethical point via an anecdote.

7. Ask for a volunteer to count the votes. As this is being done, bring closure to the exercise by raising the Discussion questions.

VARIATION
Encourage the storytellers to submit their stories to publications that deal with teamwork and other management issues.

DISCUSSION
- Do you feel it is totally ethical for someone to use research information about effective communications to make their own communications more persuasive? Why or why not?

- What are the pros and cons associated with the use of storytelling?

- What stories do you use with family members to encourage ethical behavior?

QUOTATION
"If you don't talk too good, don't talk too long."

– Ted Williams

POINTS OF INTEREST
Former New York State Governor Mario Cuomo is a master of using stories as bridges to the political points he wishes to make. He also employs metaphors: the family is one he uses often to illustrate his points. So is imagery—the vision of a shining city on a hill and the impoverished underbelly of that city, for example. Study the speeches of outstanding orators and develop a new appreciation of the power of storytelling.

If you wish to join the National Storytelling Network, you can reach them at 800-525-4514.

Handout 50.1
Teaming by Storying Around

Directions
Select the answer you believe is correct by circling the letter in front of it. Be ready to explain your answer and to provide, whenever possible, real-world examples to illustrate it or substantiate your reason for selecting it.

1. Research by J. Martin and M. Powers found that the most effective way to persuade people that a particular company was committed to avoiding layoffs was:
    (a) Telling a story
    (b) Using statistics
    (c) Using the story plus statistics
    (d) Sharing a policy statement issued by the company

2. Max DePree, former CEO of Herman Miller furniture company, asserts that every institution needs "tribal storytellers." What do you think is the purpose of such individuals?
    (a) To help ensure listening is going on
    (b) To help retain the organization's history
    (c) To help ensure the ongoing transference of values
    (d) All of the above

3. Author David Armstrong has a candy story he uses to illustrate a technique for encouraging the acceptance of change. The story involves his distributing a piece of candy to everyone at a meeting. To forestall negative comments about a change that he was proposing, Armstrong told the meeting participants, *"You are allowed one negative comment during the meeting."* After people made their comment, they had to eat their candy. Afterward, if there was no candy in front of the person, he or she was simply not permitted to attack the change being proposed. Which of these statements associated with the above story do you feel illustrates the value of the actions that constitute this story:
    (a) Disarming can be charming.
    (b) Sometimes shock treatment is called for.
    (c) If you want people to be creative, you have to be creative.
    (d) (a) and (b)
    (e) (a) and (c)
    (f) (b) and (c)
    (g) (a), (b), and (c)

Reproduced from *50 Reproducible Activities for Promoting Ethics Within the Organization*, by Marlene Caroselli. HRD Press, 2015.

References

Armstrong, David. *Managing by Storying Around*. Doubleday, 1992, pp. 135–137.

Arnold, Kristen. *Team Basics: Practical Strategies for Team Success*. QPC Press, 2000.

Beer, Michael, and Einsenstat, Russell. "The Silent Killers of Strategy Implementation and Learning." *Sloan Management Review*, Summer 2000, p. 29.

Belanger, Peter. "How to Lose Gracefully." *TeleProfessional*, January 1995, p. 52.

Brenner, Steven, and Molander, Carl. "Is the Ethics of Business Changing?" *Harvard Business Review*, January-February 1997.

Bureau of Business Practice. *Leadership and the Law*. 1996, p. 27.

Carey, Robert. "The Ethics Challenge." *Successful Meetings*, April 1998, p. 57.

Caroselli, Marlene. *The Language of Leadership*. HRD Press, 1990, p. 69.

Clement Communications. "Supervisors Need to Know." *Supervisor's Guide to Employment Practices*, 1992, p. 1.

—. "How Supervisors Can Tell If Employees Are Using Drugs." p. 3.

—. "Age-Related 'Jokes' Are Risky Business." p. 6.

DeMars, Nan. *You Want Me To Do What?* Simon and Schuster, 1997.

DePree, Max. *Leadership Is an Art*. Doubleday, 1989.

"Domestic Violence Goes to Work." *HR Manager's Legal Reporter*, pp. 1–6.

Evans, Paul. "Thrive on Paradox." *Executive Excellence*, July 2000, p. 11.

Fair, Ernest. "Room for Improvement." *Personal Selling Power*, September 1995, p. 68.

Farhi, Paul. "Captain without a Ship." *Rochester Democrat and Chronicle*, April 30, 2001, p. 1C.

Flynn, Nancy. *The ePolicy Handbook*. Amacom, 2001, p. 38

Frisch, Gerald. "Internal Investigation." *Successful Meetings*, May 1998, pp. 85–86.

Gardner, Howard. *Multiple Intelligences: The Theory and Practice*. Basic Books, 1993.

"Good Grief." *The Economist,* April 8, 1995, p. 57.

Graham, John R. "Minding Your Tongue." *Incentive,* May 1995, p. 80.

"Hardly a Successful Meeting." *Successful Meetings,* August 1992, p. 16.

Hayes, Keri. "Made in the U.S.A. (Sort of…)." *Business Ethics,* March/April 1999, p. 6.

Kahn, Jack. "A Hairy Challenge." *Incentive,* December 1997, p. 12.

Krantz, Matt, and Knox, Noelle. "Some Enron Board Members Leave Other Firms' Rosters," *USA Today,* February 11, 2002, p. 1B.

Lawrence Ragan Communications, Inc. *Positive Leadership.* Sample Issue, p. 1.

—. "Are You Guilty of Giving Your Employees an Ethical 'Flea Dip'?" p. 3.

Ley, D. Forbes. *The Best Seller.* Sales Success Press, 1990.

Mandel, Terry. "Marketing with Integrity*." Business Ethics,* September/October, 1990, p. 21.

Martin, J., and Powers, M. "Organizational Stories: More Vivid and Persuasive than Quantitative Data." *Psychological Foundations of Organizational Behavior,* edited by B. M. Staw. Scott, Foresman, 1982, pp. 161–168.

Mayer, Pam. "Profitability and the Common Good." *Leadership in Action,* Volume 17, Number 3, 1997, p. 13.

Mescon, Michael, and Mescon, Timothy. "And Then Some…" *SKY* magazine, August 1989, p. 92.

Michalko, Michael. *Thinkertoys.* Ten Speed Press, 1991.

—. *Cracking Creativity.* Ten Speed Press, 1998.

National Institute of Business Management. "The Politics of Teamwork." *The Politics of Executive Success,* 1988.

O'Boyle, Thomas. "Profit at Any Cost." *Business Ethics,* March/April 1999, pp. 13–14.

Pearson, Christine, Andersson, Lynne, and Porath, Christine. *Organizational Dynamics.* Upcoming publication of the American Management Association.

Ries, Al, and Trout, Jack. *Positioning.* Warner Books, 1993, p. 78.

Roedel, Abby, et alia. "101 Dumbest Moments in Business." *Business 2.0,* April 2002, pp. 65–74.

Royko, Mike. "No Mercy at Hospital for Grieving Couple." The Chicago *Tribune.* January 25, 1995.

"The Chicago Flood." *USA Today*, April 21, 1992, p. 10A.

Tracey, William R. "Managing the Boss." *Solutions*, March 1995, p. 55.

Ventrella, Scott. *The Power of Positive Thinking in Business.* The Free Press, 2001.

Welch, Jack. *Straight from the Gut.* Warner Business Books, 2001.